D0243170

Produced by AA Publishing
© AA Media Limited 2010

Published by AA Publishing (a trading name of AA Media Limited, whose registered office is Fanum House, Basing View, Basingstoke, Hampshire RG21 4EA; registered number 06112600)

This product includes mapping data licensed from Ordnance Survey® with the permission of the Controller of Her Majesty's Stationery Office.
© Crown copyright 2010. All rights reserved. Licence number 100021153

ISBN: 978-0-7495-6496-4
A04143

These routes appear in the AA Local Walks series and *1001 Walks in Britain*.

theAA.com/shop

Printed in China by Leo Paper Group

Picture credits
All images are held in the Automobile Association's own photo library (AA World Travel Library) and were taken by the following photographers:
Front cover T Mackie; 3 T Mackie; 6/7 T Mackie; 8 N Setchfield; 9 T Mackie; 10 T Mackie.

Opposite: Windmill at Wicken Fen, Cambridgeshire

100 WALKS IN
EASTERN ENGLAND

Contents

Eastern England

From the ancient oaks of Sherwood Forest, across the Fens to the Norfolk Broads and the North Sea coast, and up to the Lincolnshire Wolds there is a surprising variety of landscapes in the eastern side of England.

Eastern England

This region extends from the northern edge of London to the brink of Humberside. The landscape is flat and gently undulating agricultural country with prairie-like fields. The only appreciable heights are in the Lincolnshire Wolds, Bedfordshire's Dunstable Downs and Charnwood Forest in Leicestershire, but there's plenty of scenic landscape to explore.

The Great North Road seems to tie this region together, but it pays to take time to discover the surrounding landscape, and venture further east beyond Cambridgeshire and the Fens to East Anglia. The coastline from Essex up to Lowestoft is one of remote inlets and tidal estuaries. Here angry seas reclaimed Dunwich and are clawing back clifftops to the north, while farmers and weekenders alike watch their properties slip into the sea.

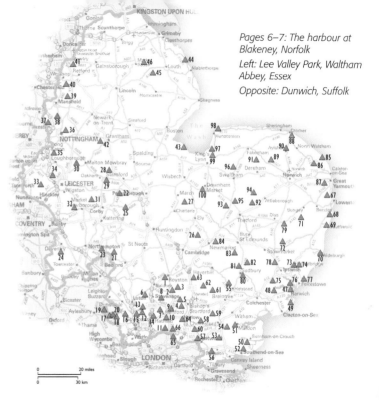

Pages 6–7: The harbour at Blakeney, Norfolk

Left: Lee Valley Park, Waltham Abbey, Essex

Opposite: Dunwich, Suffolk

Forests and Trails

Breckland is an ancient forested area that has regained its trees in comparatively modern times. Now Thetford Forest acts as a break in an otherwise monotonous landscape. Inland are villages and towns rich in medieval architecture. Before industry this was where the wealth lay, in the fertile soils, the sheep-cropped hills and grassland.

The Chiltern Ridge points a finger into the south of the region, and with it the Ridgeway National Trail and the Icknield Way follow ancient trade routes above the lowlands. The north is bounded by the National Forest, a land reclamation scheme that aims to link up surviving woodland.

Along the North Sea

With the North Sea coast forming its eastern boundary, coastal walking is one of the highlights of this region, whether you're on the edge of the tidal flats of the Wash, or negotiating the intricate maze of inlets and estuaries in east Essex.

You'll find salt marshes as you head round the coast, first to remote Paglesham, then to the Dengie Peninsula and the ancient chapel at Bradwell on Sea. This is an Essex you won't see unless you

walk – to the windswept marshes of Walton-on-the-Naze or in the bracing seaside air of Harwich. The Suffolk estuaries of the Orwell and the Deben will remind you of Essex, but by the time you pass the shingle spit of Orford Ness, you will know you are in a different place. Aldeburgh inspired composer Benjamin Britten, and Southwold is a genteel resort.

One for the Birds

East Anglians are most proud of the North Norfolk coast. Here the towns and fishing villages play a secondary role to the bird reserves that line the northern shore.

From Overstrand in the east to Snettisham in the west lie miles of dunes, beaches and mud flats, which provide a vital resting area for migrant birds. Perhaps the marshland at Blakeney is most famous, but don't overlook the stretch from Holme-next-the-Sea to the Burnhams. The walking is easy, the birdspotting easier still. This stretch of coast is made accessible by the North Norfolk Coast Path National Trail.

More Trails

The Peddars Way is an ancient trade route and you'll come across it many times in Norfolk. At Castle Acre it dissects a Norman castle mound on one side and a medieval priory on the other. On the edge of Thetford Forest you can follow a section of the Way in conjunction with the Great Eastern Pingo Trail. This stretch of disused railway cuts an easy line across a strange post-glacial landscape.

Writers and Artists

Some of the nation's leading writers and artists have drawn their inspiration here. Constable has become synonymous with East Bergholt in Suffolk; D H Lawrence drew heavily on his upbringing in the mining town of Eastwood.

Defenders of the triangle of greenbelt around Ayot St Lawrence remind us of the contribution George Bernard Shaw made to the nation's heritage.

Woodland Walking

You will also find some rewarding woodland walks. Around Thetford Forest there are several trails which make pleasing circuits. This is modern commercial forest, but despite this, the wildlife abounds. Sherwood Forest is perhaps one of the most famous in the world, though this once great area of wild wood has been reduced to a pocket of oaks and some larger areas of conifer plantation in north Nottinghamshire. There are opportunities here to glimpse the woodland cover of old at Clumber Park and Newstead Abbey.

In Leicestershire the National Forest has taken over sites that had been scarred by collieries. The ambitious planting scheme is accompanied by well-marked trails and has included a return of broadleaved woodland to the area.

In Northamptonshire, you'll find the remnants of Rockingham Forest, another royal hunting ground. The remaining fragments around Fineshade Abbey, now in the hands of the Forestry Commission, form the centrepiece of plans to reintroduce the red kite to the East Midlands. In Hertfordshire, the National Trust has done much to preserve the beech woodlands of Ashridge, cloaking the northerly reaches of the Chilterns.

A Touch of Artifice

At Wicken Fen a wetland habitat has been preserved and slowly expanded. At Manea and Gedney Drove End you'll see how the draining of the Fens has affected the area's ecology. In the Broads, it was the flooding that followed centuries of peat extraction that created a unique wetland habitat. The flooding of a river valley system in Rutland created one of the largest artificial lakes in Europe, and a stroll around the newly created Hambleton Peninsula is included.

Using this Book

❶ Information panels

Information panels show the total distance and total amount of ascent (that is the accumulated height you will ascend throughout the walk). An indication of the gradient you will encounter is shown by the rating 0–3. Zero indicates fairly flat ground and 3 indicates undulating terrain with several very steep slopes.

❷ Minimum time

The minimum time suggested is for approximate guidance only. It assumes reasonably fit walkers and doesn't allow for stops.

❸ Start points

The start of each walk is given as a six-figure grid reference prefixed by two letters indicating which 100km square of the National Grid it refers to. You'll find more information on grid references on most Ordnance Survey maps.

4 Abbreviations

Walk directions use these abbreviations:

L – left

L–H – left-hand

R – right

R–H – right-hand

Names which appear on signposts are given in brackets, for example ('Bantam Beach').

5 Suggested maps

Details of appropriate maps are given for each walk, and usually refer to 1:25,000 scale Ordnance Survey Explorer maps. We strongly recommend that you always take the appropriate OS map with you. The maps in this book are there to give you the route and do not show all the details or relief that you will need to navigate around the routes provided in this collection. You can purchase Ordnance Survey Explorer maps at all good bookshops.

6 Car parking

Many of the car parks suggested are public, but occasionally you may find you have to park on the roadside or in a lay-by. Please be considerate when you leave your car, ensuring that access roads or gates are not blocked and that other vehicles can pass safely. Remember that pub car parks are private and should not be used unless you are visiting the pub or you have the landlord's permission to park there.

Opposite: A detail of the ancient Guildhall in Lavenham, Suffolk

---

00

LOCATION Walk title

From the tops of Bulbarrow Hill to the valley floor and back, via an atmospheric church.

4.25 miles/6.8km 2hrs **Ascent** 591ft/180m ⚠ **Difficulty** 1

Paths Quiet roads, muddy bridleways, field paths, 2 stiles

Map OS Explorer 117 Cerne Abbas & Bere Regis **Grid ref** ST 791071

Parking Car park at Ibberton Hill picnic site

County • REGION

112

1 Turn **L** along road, following Wessex Ridgeway, with Ibberton laid out below to **R**. Road climbs gradually, and you see masts on Bulbarrow Hill ahead.

2 After 1 mile (1.6km) pass car park on **L**, with plaque about Thomas Hardy. At junction bear **R** and immediately **R** again, signposted 'Stoke Wake'. Pass another car park on **R**. Woods of Woolland Hill now fall away steeply on **R**. Pass radio masts to **L** and reach small gate into field on **R**, near end of wood. Before taking it, go extra few steps to road junction ahead for wonderful view of escarpment stretching away west.

3 Go through gate and follow uneven bridleway down. Glimpse spring-fed lake through trees on R. At bottom of field, path swings **L** to gate. Go through, on to road. Turn **R**, continuing downhill. Follow road into Woolland, passing Manor House and Old Schoolhouse, on **L** and **R** respectively.

4 Beyond entrance, on **L**, to Woolland House turn **R** into lane and immediately **L** through kissing

gate. Path immediately forks. Take **L-H** track, down through marshy patches and young sycamores. Posts with yellow footpath waymarkers lead straight across meadow, with gorse-clad Chitcombe Down up **R**. Cross footbridge over stream. Go straight on to cross road. Keeping straight on, go through hedge gap. Bear **L** down field, cross stile and continue down. Cross footbridge and stile to continue along **L** side of next field. Go through gate to road junction. Walk straight up road ahead and follow it **R**, into Ibberton. Bear **R**.

5 Continue up this road through village. This steepens and becomes path, bearing **R**. Steps lead up to church. Continue up steep path. Cross road and go straight ahead through gate. Keep straight on along fence, climbing steadily. Cross under power lines, continue in same direction, climbing steadily. Carry on open pasture to small gate in hedge. Do not go through gate, but turn sharp **L**, up slope, to small gate opposite car park.

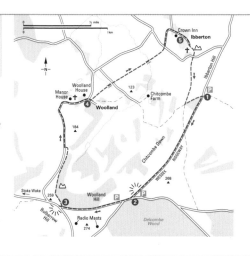

Crown Inn
Ibberton

Woolland House

Manor House

Chitcombe Farm

Woolland

123

184

Chitcombe Down

268

Stoke Wake

259

Woolland Hill

Bulbarrow Hill

Radio Masts

274

Delcombe Wood

1

THERFIELD Fair On The Dewey Downs
A walk between Therfield and Kelshall along winding lanes.

3.5 miles/5.7km 1hr 30min **Ascent** 120ft/36m ⚠ **Difficulty** 1
Paths Green lanes, tracks, field paths, village lanes
Map OS Explorer 194 Hertford & Bishop's Stortford **Grid ref** TL 335370
Parking Around Therfield village green

❶ From village green walk down Church Lane and into parish churchyard. Go through gap in railings to south of south porch on to green lane, with vicarage garden on **L** and field on **R**. At footpath post keep straight on along grassy margin at **L** of field, then go across field to kissing gate. Cross pasture to gate, go through this and turn **R** into green lane, Duck's Green. Ignoring footpaths **R** and **L**, track bears **L**, now following parish boundary. Where path meets track, turn **R** into green lane.
❷ Follow lane, which soon turns **R**, climbing gently between ancient hedges. At track junction go **L** and continue climbing, passing footpath junction before reaching crest of hill. Ignore track turning **L** – carry straight on along loosely metalled track.
❸ Further on turn **R** on to bridleway, with fence and paddocks **L**, arable land **R**. This becomes track through arable land. At bridleway post, where hedge reappears, turn **R** into green lane, soon hedged only on **L**. At

post-and-railed sheep enclosure go **L**. Then, through gate, turn **L** to another gate into lane and cross to church lychgate.
❹ Visit Church of St Faith, entering through its original, heavy, 15th-century door. Leave churchyard from behind chancel on to path between fence and walls, signposted 'Hertfordshire Way'. At lane turn **L**. At road junction jink **R** then **L** to walk past telephone box and village hall (1895).
❺ Continue past Fox Hall Farm and pond. Turn **R** at footpath sign, just before thatched cottage, on to track initially between hedges, then alongside patchy hedge. At end of field go through hedge and over footbridge. Turn sharp **L** to walk round 2 sides of small field. At track go **L** to walk past tall water tower. At road turn **R** and follow it past Tuthill Court and Victorian estate cottages. Turn **R** past Bell House into Pedlars Lane, which winds back to Therfield village green.

Hertfordshire • EASTERN ENGLAND

12

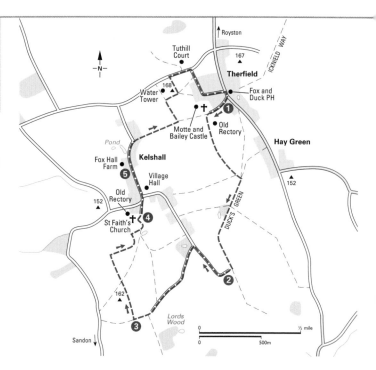

BUNTINGFORD A Medieval Market

Visit the old parish church, Wyddial village and return past manor houses.

8 miles/12.9km 3hrs **Ascent** 120ft/37m ⚠ **Difficulty** 2
Paths Tracks, lanes, field paths, village roads
Map OS Explorer 194 Hertford & Bishop's Stortford **Grid ref** TL 360295
Parking Buntingford High Street car park

❶ From car park cross road and turn into Church Street. Descend past Fox and Duck pub. Go **L** into Wyddial Road, then **R** across River Rib ford into The Causeway. Lane leaves town and becomes winding rural lane. Beneath canopy of trees turn **R** to visit remains of St Bartholomew's Church.

❷ From churchyard continue along green lane downhill to road. Turn **R** and follow road uphill. At bend go **L** at bridleway sign, path being grassy baulk between arable fields. At road go straight on and wind through Wyddial to parish church.

❸ From churchyard continue along road to bend. Turn **R**, by footpath sign, to walk along **R** side of hedge. Cross footbridge and then turn **L**. Continue east, first on **R-H** side of hedge, then via footbridge on **L**, to farm access road. Turn **R** along this and walk to Beauchamps.

❹ Route passes to **L** of Beauchamps, initially alongside neat hedge, then bears **L** off concrete track on to grassy track, with poplars on **R**. Continue to track at brow of hill and turn **R**. Past Beauchamp's Wood track

gradually descends to valley floor before turning **L** and gently ascending to next crest. Turn **R** beside concrete hardstanding. Descending gradually, follow metalled track to **L**.

❺ At road cross on to drive to Alswick Hall. Passing pond and farm buildings, then hall itself, route follows green lane to Owles Hall.

❻ Beyond Owles Hall turn **R** on to lane. Descend westwards, to cross valley of Haley Hill Ditch. Next, ascend towards Buntingford, with Sainsbury's distribution centre to **L**. At end of Owles Lane turn **R** to walk along Roman Ermine Street.

❼ Turn **L** past The Railway pub into Aspenden Road, then go **R** into Luynes Rise. At footpath sign go **R**, tarmac path winding beside River Rib, with modern housing on **L**. Keep **R** at fork and beyond cottages path emerges into High Street. Turn **L**, passing St Peter's Church and Seth Ward Almshouses, to start.

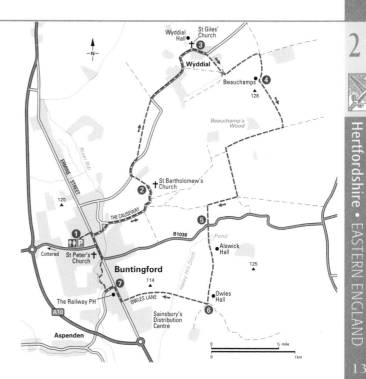

3

GREAT HORMEAD Rich With Corn

A walk round Great and Little Hormead, east of the young River Quin.

4 miles/6.4km 2hrs **Ascent** 85ft/26m ⚠ **Difficulty** ☐1

Paths Field paths, tracks, quiet country lanes, village road, 6 stiles

Map OS Explorer 194 Hertford & Bishop's Stortford **Grid ref** TL 402298

Parking Horseshoe Hill, Great Hormead

❶ Start on Horseshoe Hill, a turning just west of Three Tuns pub. Uphill, bear **R** at war memorial, and follow lane to St Nicholas', parish church of Great Hormead. From churchyard continue along lane, turning **L** at junction that is signposted to Little Hormead and Furneux Pelham. Pass Little Hormead Bury Farm, its barns converted to houses, and reach Norman parish church of Little Hormead.

❷ Continue along lane. Opposite Bulls Farm go **L** at footpath sign into cultivated land, following hedges north through 2 fields, then go **L** and **R** alongside hedge to junction. Carry straight on along track. At first byway, this becomes footpath across fields to main street of Great Hormead.

❸ Turn **R** on to road. Go beyond **L** turn, Hall Lane. When opposite thatched barn go to **L** of chevron-style bend sign to inconspicuous start of footpath. This follows course of Black Ditch stream, sometimes on **L**, sometimes on **R**, stream and hedge eventually bearing

L. Cross stream on bridge into pasture and head for footpath post at lane.

❹ Turn **L** to walk along lane, initially with hedge on **L** only, then on both sides. The lane continues winding gently downhill – you will see an electricity pylon on the **L**. Pass beneath its cables to go **L** at footpath sign on to track, with hedge **R** Over the brow descend towards Hormead Hall. Go **R** of cattle grid to stile, then head diagonally **L** across pasture to another stile.

❺ Cross. Go **L** along edge of arable field. Look **L** here, through hedge, to see the remains of Hormead Hall's medieval moat. Turn **L** out of field, then turn **R** along Hall Lane, to road junction. Turn **R** into Hormead Road, main street of Great Hormead. **L** turn past Three Tuns pub returns you to Horseshoe Hill.

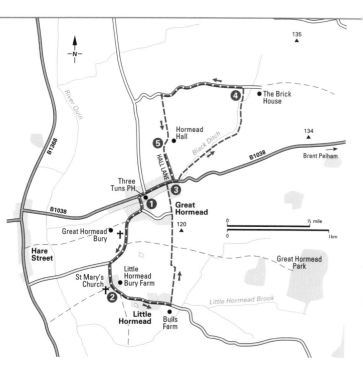

Hertfordshire • EASTERN ENGLAND

MUCH HADHAM Gorgeous Palace, Solemn Temple

Through a lovely village.

4.5 miles/7.2km 2hrs 30min **Ascent** 115ft/35m ⚠ **Difficulty** ☐1

Paths Field paths and tracks, 5 stiles

Map OS Explorer 194 Hertford & Bishop's Stortford

Grid ref TL 428197 **Parking** North end of High Street, just south of B1004 **L** turn

❶ Walk along High Street into village, going **R** just before war memorial, over stile beside ball-finialled gate piers. Follow drive, then go **L** to stile at corner of tennis courts. Now in parkland to Moor Place, head diagonally to skirt **L** of farm buildings. Then go to **R-H** corner of wood and join farm access track. Cross drive on to metalled track, then bear **L** along granite slabway to kissing gate beside Dell Cottage.

❷ Cross over road to footpath signed 'Windmill Way' and cross arable field, heading to **L** of rendered cottage. Follow track behind gardens to road, keep **R** and bear **R** again past telephone box, route becoming metalled lane and later hedgeless track amid cultivated land. Where this swings **L**, carry straight on to valley floor, bearing **R** at cottages, still along field edge. At corner of woodland keep **R** towards Camwell Hall, attractive 15th-century hall house.

❸ At farm bear **L** on to its access drive, which becomes lane, passing Wynches, early 19th-century stucco villa on **L** Turn **R** on to B1004 to descend to Hadham Mill. Turn

L at lane after crossing bridge over River Ash.

❹ Follow lane and go **L** through gate with bridleway and Hertfordshire Way signs. Turn **R** along track and then bear **L**. Follow this delightful, well-waymarked path, with steeply sloping woods to **R** and river **L**. Eventually reach lane.

❺ Go **L** here and follow lane to turn **L** at T-junction by Sidehill House. At kissing gate go **R**, signed 'Hertfordshire Way', to walk along floor of pastoral valley with River Ash to **L**. At lane go straight on, then **R** at 'Public Footpath 21' sign over River Ash. Climb steeply through copse. Turn **L** on to metalled lane, wooded river cliff now **L**.

❻ Just before road junction go **L** at public footpath sign. Bear **L** (not straight on) to descend steeply on holloway track through woods down to river. Cross footbridge and follow path to churchyard.

❼ Visit St Andrew's Church. From churchyard you can get an excellent view of the Bishop's Palace. Continue westwards, back to the High Street.

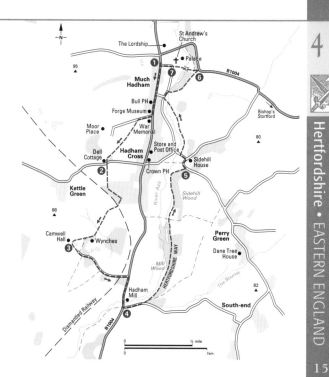

5

Hertfordshire • EASTERN ENGLAND

16

LITTLE HADHAM Royal Associations
Circuit of picturesque 'ends' and hamlets of Little Hadham and out to Hadham Hall.

4 miles/6.4km 1hr 45min **Ascent** 125ft/100m ⚠ **Difficulty** 1

Paths Field paths, tracks, roads and village pavements, 2 stiles

Map OS Explorer 194 Hertford & Bishop's Stortford **Grid ref** TL 440228

Parking Albury Road, Little Hadham (north of traffic lights at A120 crossroads)

❶ Walk uphill on Albury Road, to footpath sign on **R** 'To Church 0.5 and Bishop's Stortford 2.75'. Take this path alongside arable field, which descends to River Ash, here merely small stream. Cross footbridge to climb on to grassy baulk between fields. This leads to church, whose tower peeps from churchyard surrounded by trees.

❷ Leave churchyard with many-gabled rear of Church End farmhouse on **R** to enter lane. Go **L**, past old church hall (now converted to bungalow). Follow track round to **R** of farm buildings to climb to brow of hill. At public bridleway junction-post turn **R**. Modern development of houses (Baud Close) stands behind fine brick-built barn, now house.

❸ From central grassed courtyard of Hadham Hall and its outbuildings, pass 1570s gatehouse to walk down lime avenue to A120 (Roman Stane Street). Turn **R** and shortly turn **L** down Millfield Lane. Junction is highest point on walk.

❹ Beyond Millfield Cottage go **R**, on to metalled green lane by public byway sign where lane turns **L**. At a fork go **R**, still on hedged green lane. Passing splendidly named Muggins Wood, climb to lane. Turn **R** and follow lane, descending into Hadham Ford.

❺ At junction, with war memorial in small triangular green, turn **R** along main street. Lane crosses river. At public footpath sign opposite Nag's Head pub turn to **R** across footbridge leading to stile.

❻ Over stile turn **L** and head for **L-H** corner of wood, modest river on **L**. Continue uphill, keeping trees on **R** and at large field with woods on horizon, swing **L** between arable fields with St Cecelia's Church in Little Hadham visible ahead. Path passes paddocks on **L**, then jinks past primary school, emerging on to A120 past single-storey thatched cottage.

❼ Turn **L** along pavement, past school, to traffic lights. Cross river bridge to group of buildings at staggered central crossroads. Turn **R** here, back into Albury Road.

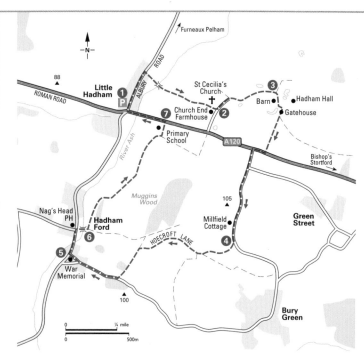

KINGSWALDEN PARK Manners And Mansions

A walk in rolling hills between Preston and Kingswalden with its former deer park.

5 miles/8km 2hrs 30min **Ascent** 115ft/35m ⚠ **Difficulty** 1
Paths Mix of field paths, green lanes and village lanes, 3 stiles
Map OS Explorer 193 Luton & Stevenage **Grid ref** TL 180247
Parking Preston village green, near Red Lion pub

❶ From village green walk down Hitchin Road and turn **L** into Chequers Lane. Beyond Chequers Cottages go **L** at footpath sign. Reach lane; go briefly **L**, then **R** at another footpath sign, to head diagonally **R** through pasture. Passing between shelter shed and Pond Farm, bear **L** and follow field path across fields to kissing gate in **R** corner. Here turn **R** on to green lane, parish boundary between Preston and King's Walden. Follow it uphill to **L** turn on to another green lane, which curves **L**. Follow it downhill. Reaching tarmac lane turn **R**.
❷ Near Wantsend Farm turn **L** into Plough Lane, which curves uphill. Just before Plough pub go **R**, over 2 stiles. Path reaches lane through playground. Out of this turn **R** to road, then **L** past School House and **L** again, signed 'Offley, King's Walden'. At road junction bear **R** to footpath sign beside de-restriction sign.
❸ Turn **L** on to this footpath, descending alongside winding hedge. Turn sharp **L** to pass modern farm building. Follow track until it turns **L** – here your path

turns **R**, along edge of wood. Turn **L** at next footpath post. At end of field turn **R** into lane to descend to King's Walden Church.
❹ From churchyard glimpse Kingswalden Bury. Retrace steps uphill, past yew hedge, and at footpath on **R**, signposted 'Frogmore', turn **R** into Kingswalden Park. Cross lime avenue to superb stretch of deer park. Go diagonally **R**. Just beyond oak, at footpath post, bear **L** towards house with big gable, outside park. Leave deer park through kissing gate. Turn **R** on to lane. Turn **L** at junction past Whitehall Farm.
❺ At footpath sign go **R** by modern farmbuilding, then go diagonally **L**, descending across arable land and keeping **R** of Whitehall Wood. Across lane route climbs on path, then runs alongside hedges and through paddock to reach lane. Here turn **L**. At junction turn **R**. At boundary wall of Temple Dinsley park, now home to Princess Helena College, turn **L**, back to Preston village green.

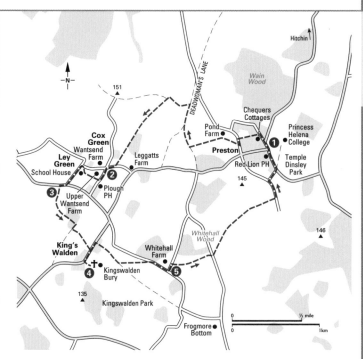

TEWIN Along Water-Meadows
The Mimram Valley and Queen Hoo Hall.

6 miles/9.7km 2hrs 45min **Ascent** 225ft/69m ⚠ **Difficulty** 2

Paths Bridleways, field paths through water-meadows, lanes, 1 stile

Map OS Explorer 182 St Albans & Hatfield **Grid ref** TL 271156

Parking On roadside around Lower Green, Tewin, opposite Tewin Memorial Hall

❶ From Lower Green turn **L** into School Lane, then **R** at footpath sign to Digswell. Across arable fields track merges from **R**. Ignore footpath crossroads, going next **L** into lane. Turn **L** at junction and shortly go **R** to isolated St Peter's Church.

❷ From churchyard descend to valley floor and turn **R**. Path bears **R**; turn **L** on to track. Where it veers **L** carry straight on, along field edge to merge with lane. Keep on lane to River Mimram bridge.

❸ Across bridge climb stile on **L** to permissive path in water-meadows alongside Mimram. At single-arch bridge cross river; leave water-meadows via kissing gate.

❹ Go straight across farmland to enter scrub belt, becoming parkland to Marden Hill. Cross lime avenue (look **L** to mansion) then follow drive to road.

❺ Across road walk alongside oak woods. Where track curves **R** go through gate into paddocks and out via kissing gate. Cross cultivated ground to reach track. Follow this past remains of Westend Farm to hornbeams

of Park Wood and turn **R** along its edge.

❻ Path jinks out to pass Bramfieldbury, then cuts across fields to its access lane. Follow this into Bramfield and turn **R** to church.

❼ From Bramfield churchyard turn **R** into recreation ground and then **L** to retrace steps past village hall to valley floor. Here turn **R**, signposted 'Beal's Wood'. Cross arable ground to corner of wood. Path goes through woods with some waymarker posts. Cross several footbridges and bear **R** at waymark to pass alongside pheasant inclosures. Turn **R** at next track T-junction. At pole barrier go **R** and emerge from woods on to track across more cultivated land.

❽ Pass superb 1580s Queen Hoo Hall. At lane turn **L** and follow winding lane down Tewin Hill into Tewin.

❾ At main road turn **R**. Pass Plume of Feathers pub to Upper Green, and go **L** along edge of green to footpath behind scrub. Pass pond to metalled green lane and follow this, eventually curving **L** back to Lower Green.

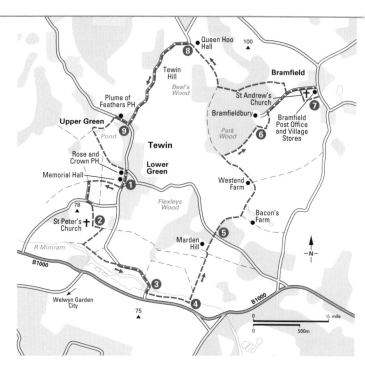

BEANE VALLEY Walking The Valley

To Walkern and its castle.

6 miles/9.7km 2hrs 45min **Ascent** 165ft/50m ⚠ **Difficulty** 2
Paths Field paths, bridleways, village roads, 3 stiles
Map OS Explorers 193 Luton & Stevenage; 194 Hertford & Bishop's Stortford
Grid ref TL 297235 (on Explorer 193) **Parking** On roadside near Benington's parish church

❶ Walk past entrance to Lordship Gardens. At green bear **L**, passing Old School Green. Before bend go **R** on to bridleway. Go **L** of gates to Walkern Hall. Passing horse paddocks to **L** and stucco hall to **R**, reach lane and turn **R**.

❷ Immediately past Walkern Hall Farm turn **L** to leave lane for bridleway signed 'Bassus Green'. Continue past farm buildings on track to stream. Ascend, with woods to **R** curving **R** to lane. At lane go **L** to Bassus Green and straight on at crossroads, on to farm access lane.

❸ At Walkern Bury Farm turn **L**. By byway sign turn **R** on to track to descend into valley bottom. Here turn **L** on to green lane. Follow this muddy lane into Walkern.

❹ From church cross River Beane on footbridge, then turn **L** through kissing gate into pasture. Beyond farm buildings head diagonally to kissing gate and thence to road. Turn **L** into Walkern High Street to walk through village, keeping ahead at junction signposted 'Benington'.

❺ Out of village, where road bears **L**, go through gate and immediately **L** to gate along track. Through kissing gate this is start of 1 mile (1.6km) walk along Beane Valley, river winding on **L**. At footpath junction, where river swings **R**, cross it on modern footbridge.

❻ Now head between arable fields towards woodlands on ridge ahead. Cross road (to footpath signposted 'Benington 1') and climb to woods. After these pass through Lordship Farm – follow waymarker arrows painted on buildings – on to often very muddy track. Continue into cattle-grazed pasture and keep **R** when track forks, to galvanised gate. Across footbridge path bears **R** in more pasture to bypass Benington Bury (house) to gate in far corner. Path skirts Lordship Gardens on **R** and sheep pasture on **L** to Walkern Road. Turn **R**, back to green and St Peter's Church.

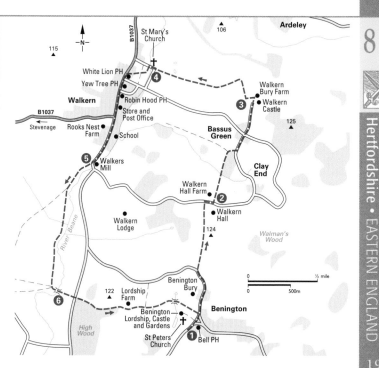

THUNDRIDGE Heroes And Pioneers

Explore a pagan settlement at Thundridge.

4 miles/6.4km 2hrs **Ascent** 140ft/43m ⚠ **Difficulty** ☐1

Paths Good paths and tracks with only one large arable field to cross, no stiles

Map OS Explorer 194 Hertford & Bishop's Stortford **Grid ref** TL 359172

Parking Ermine Street, Thundridge (to east of A10)

❶ At bend in Ermine Street are 2 footpath signs: follow 'Ware' sign steeply uphill to Victorian parish churchyard, for good views. Retrace your steps downhill to Ermine Street and follow other footpath, signposted 'Thundridge Old Church'. After kissing gate go straight on across pasture, now on Hertfordshire Way, then cross arable land to descend to Rib Valley. Turn **R** on to tarmac path. Pass under A10 Wadesmill bypass, heading for Cold Christmas. Once under road, turn **L** on to path. Ruined church tower is visible ahead and to **L**, beyond river, are grounds of Youngsbury, country house from 1745 set in 'Capability' Brown parkland.

❷ Only tower of medieval parish church remains. Continue along metalled track, between pastures. Pass tree-lined track on **R** and continue straight ahead onfootpath. Cross an access road. At footpath crossroads go **L** over footbridge that bypasses River Rib ford.

❸ Now climb out of valley with arable fields to **R**, Youngsbury's parkland to **L**. At brow track skirts woodland (arboretum). Carry straight on, ignoring track bearing **R**. Go straight on, past farm buildings. Track, now metalled, curves **L** and downhill.

❹ Reaching white-painted, iron gates, ignore path on **R** and continue along metalled road to recross old A10 before arriving in High Cross. Turn **R** at village street to visit High Cross Church.

❺ From churchyard turn **L** down A10, here following course of Ermine Street. Near White Horse pub turn **R** into Marshall's Lane. Pass modern houses, then Marshall's Farm and Marshall's (both Victorian), to descend into valley by winding holloway lane.

❻ Cross The Bourne and go **L** by footpath signposted 'Wadesmill' (footpath is to **L**, not field track on **R**). Path keeps alongside The Bourne almost into Wadesmill where it crosses to other bank on footbridge. It becomes gravelled access lane and you reach main road.

❼ Turn **R** over River Rib bridge. Turn **L** at Post Office Stores of 1904, back into Ermine Street, Thundridge.

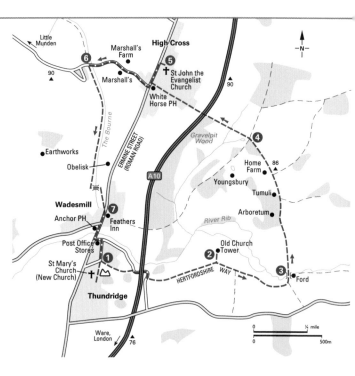

HERTFORD HEATH Great Wells At Great Amwell

From Hertford Heath.

6.5 miles/10.4km 2hrs 30min **Ascent** 200ft/61m ⚠ **Difficulty** 2
Paths Bridleways, field paths and canal tow path, 4 stiles
Map OS Explorer 174 Epping Forest & Lee Valley **Grid ref** TL 350116
Parking Green at Church Hill or Mount Pleasant Road, Hertford Heath, off B1197

❶ Walk east along Mount Pleasant and by Mount Pleasant sign take **L** fork along metalled track.
❷ At end bridleway bears **R** on to wooded heath, then **L** at bridleway post. Descend through hornbeam and oak woods, marked by occasional waymarker posts. As it becomes sunken lane, bear **R** out of wood, then **L**. Cross access lane, go **L** and descend alongside embankment of A10.
❸ Go under A10, turning **L** up to stile, signposted 'Walnut Tree Walk'. Continue alongside A10 to high, chain-link gate. Go through this to ascend alongside conifer belt and reach metalled lane at crest. Turn **R**.
❹ At next road, with garden centre on **R**, turn **L** by Gothic-windowed Amwellbury Lodge. Shortly turn **R** into Church Path and follow footpath to Great Amwell.
❺ Pass George IV pub and turn **R** into churchyard. From churchyard descend steps, cross lane and descend further, to New River – Myddelton Monument urn island is **L**. Turn **R** to follow New River footpath, shortly passing Amwell Marsh Pumping Station.

❻ Leave New River at road, turning **R**, uphill. Past Hillside Lane go **L** to restricted byway sign. Track runs between fields, over A414, and continues to A1170. Cross this and go over stile into pasture. Climb to crest, go over 1st stile then 2nd and turn **R** to descend to A10 roundabout.
❼ Turn **L** under A10, cross to byway sign and go **L** up bank. At top turn **R** to walk alongside woods, now in grounds of Haileybury College. Continue straight on past end of woods on track.
❽ At crossroads continue along tarmac drive, with Haileybury College on **L**. College road merges with B1197. Turn **L** at College Arms, soon with scrubby heathland of The Roundings on **R**. Where road bears **L** just before large white house (Meadow Grange), fork **R** on to heath, through trees, to bear **L** onto grassy path. Follow this to road and turn **R** on to track.
❾ Now on Roman Ermine Street, follow it northwards to merge with B1197 through Hertford Heath. At Country Stores shop turn **R** into Church Hill and back to green.

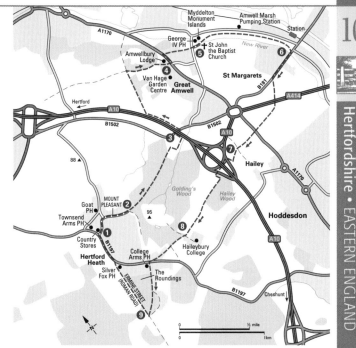

CHESHUNT A Peaceful Oasis

A walk from the centre of Cheshunt, taking in construction, demolition and removal.

6 miles/9.7km 2hrs 45min **Ascent** 130ft/40m ⚠ **Difficulty** 2

Paths Lanes, footpaths, field and river paths, 6 stiles

Map OS Explorer 174 Epping Forest & Lee Valley **Grid ref** TL 349023

Parking Churchgate, Cheshunt, east of church near Green Dragon

❶ From Churchgate cross churchyard and leave by far corner. Pass to **R** of St Mary's School, on path initially between fences, then playing fields. At road go **L**, then **L** again into Dark Lane. Beyond Cromwell Avenue, pass between cemeteries into Bury Green Road.

❷ Just past No 104 turn **R**, on to footpath. Go along cul-de-sac and turn **L** at T-junction, almost immediately turning **R**, footpath signed 'Barrow Lane'. At bypass path goes **R**, to road bridge.

❸ Over bridge turn **L** along Broadfield Farm's access road. Turn **L** at farmyard gate, skirt farm buildings and descend to cross Theobalds Brook. Now ascend **R** side of 2 fields. Go through 2 gates in quick succession and then turn immediately **R**, along edge of fields towards woods. Skirt these, **L** then **R**, to join track by Theobalds Estate Yard and turn **L** on to lane.

❹ Veer **R** after few paces to follow waymarked path. At woods path goes along **L** side and crosses M25.

Descending to stile and footbridge, follow line of oaks through pasture. At its corner go **R** over bridge, path then skirting stables towards King and Tinker pub.

❺ Turn **L** along Whitewebbs Lane and turn **L** opposite White Webbs Centre on to Bulls Cross Ride, signposted 'Western Cemetery'.

❻ Across M25 follow lane past Western Cemetery, bearing **L** at gates to Theobalds. At T-junction go **R**, on to bridleway, initially alongside walls of Theobalds' kitchen gardens, then along green lane curving **L**.

❼ Past Temple Bar, continue to Cheshunt bypass. Across it, go **R** over stile into wood. Continue into paddocks, then through gate by bridge over New River.

❽ Turn **L** along tow path. Walk past housing estates and leave New River at road bridge. Turn **L** and then **R** into Churchgate, passing borough offices to church.

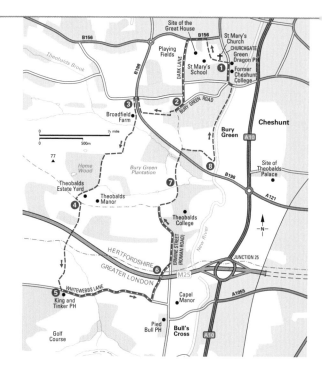

WHEATHAMPSTEAD Where Julius Caesar Marched

In the footsteps of the Roman legions.

5 miles/8km 2hrs **Ascent** 155ft/47m ⚠ **Difficulty** 1
Paths Field paths, bridleway tracks and lanes
Map OS Explorer 182 St Albans & Hatfield **Grid ref** TL 178141
Parking East Lane car park, Wheathampstead

❶ Turn **R** past Bull, go over River Lea bridge; turn **R** into Mount Road. At bridleway sign follow track, waymarked 'Ayot Green'. You will emerge in open countryside to wind alongside river.

❷ Go through gate with bypass embankment ahead, and turn **R**. Go between fences and pass through another gate, then bear **R** on to metalled track, re-crossing Lea. Now on Sheepcote Lane, go uphill, over main road into Dyke Lane.

❸ By Tudor Road go **L** on to footpath along remarkably deep ditch of Devil's Dyke. Emerging at lane, turn **L** and follow it, then go **R** at footpath sign opposite Beech Hyde Farm. Now on grass track amid arable fields, pass modern housing to **R**, to reach road.

❹ Cross road to footpath signposted 'Nomansland', and turn **L** on to tarmac track –road runs parallel, to **L**. Walk downhill to Wicked Lady pub and turn **R** on to access drive to Wheathampstead Cricket Club. Pass behind pavilion to footpath. Turn **L** past some cricket nets, and continue through woods, keeping cricket

ground visible over to **L** through trees. Make for far end of wood by gorse bushes and bench. Bear **R** here to 2nd bench and head straight on for road.

❺ At Nomansland car park turn **R** into Down Green Lane, which leads off common. At crossroads carry straight on, past Elephant and Castle pub.

❻ Shortly, opposite Weavers Cottage, go **L** at footpath sign and up few steps. Path passes golf course, then crosses cultivated land to road, Pipers Lane. Turn **R**.

❼ At T-junction go straight across, heading diagonally **L** across pasture to stile and **R** on to track. Turn immediately **R** on to muddy track which shortly turns **L** downhill between horse fences, then **R**. After about 1 mile (1.6km) housing appears on **L**, path becomes tarmac and jinks to road.

❽ Go **L** into High Meads and then **R** to descend into Wheathampstead. At Bury Green go **L** to church. From churchyard go **L** into High Street and end of walk.

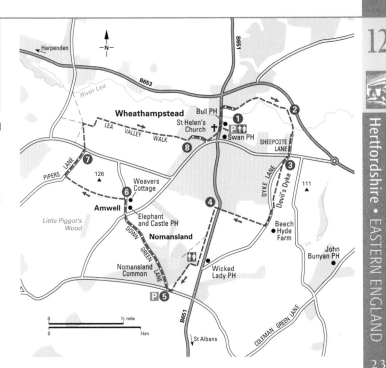

AYOT ST LAWRENCE Shaw Corner
Past the home of George Bernard Shaw.

5 miles/8km 2hrs **Ascent** 120ft/37m ⚠ **Difficulty** ☐1

Paths Bridleways, former railway line and field paths, 1 stile **Map** OS Explorer 182 St Albans & Hatfield
Grid ref TL 195168 **Parking** Roadside parking in Ayot St Lawrence near the Brocket Arms

❶ From roadside near Brocket Arms, head west past ruined Church of St Lawrence and, at bend, go to **R** of phone box through kissing gate. Portico of old church should be ahead. Now in pasture, take **R-H** fork path, with post-and-wire fence to **R**. Enter another kissing gate and cross pasture grazed by sheep to St Lawrence's 'new' church, entering churchyard via 3rd kissing gate.
❷ Leave churchyard from behind church, along metalled access drive. At lane go **R**, signposted 'Hertfordshire Way', then go **L** past timber-framed cottage into pasture. Descend steps to path along edge of wood. Turn **L** to follow it, passing leafy grounds of Shaw Corner, to reach road.
❸ Turn **R** and soon, where road swings to **R**, go straight on at public bridleway sign. Follow bridleway, which is narrow, high-hedged and often muddy green lane. At summit bypass footpath through scrub avoids muddiest parts of bridleway. Go through wooded kissing gate and follow path as it winds amid belt of beautiful oak and hornbeam trees to road via kissing gate.

❹ At road, jink **L** then **R** to public bridleway sign. Walk alongside oak and hornbeam coppiced woodland. Through conifer copse path emerges, now in arable field, with hedge to **L**. Ahead of you is embankment of old Hatters Line railway.
❺ Go **R** at railway bridge to climb embankment and then **L**, back across bridge. Follow old trackbed until just before start of woods. Here go **L** over stile. Bear **R**, ignoring **L-H** path, and follow path along edge of woodland.
❻ At road go **R** to visit Ayot St Peter church. Retrace steps past former school and continue along lane until it turns sharp **L** at cemetery. You go straight on to grassy track **L** of Tamarisk Cottage. Follow the bridleway, much of it hedgeless track between arable fields, cross road and continue on bridleway.
❼ Pass through hedge to lane opposite Stocking Lane Cottage and turn **R** uphill to road junction. At Lord Mead Lane go **L**, signposted 'Shaw Corner' and bear **L** back to Brocket Arms pub and start.

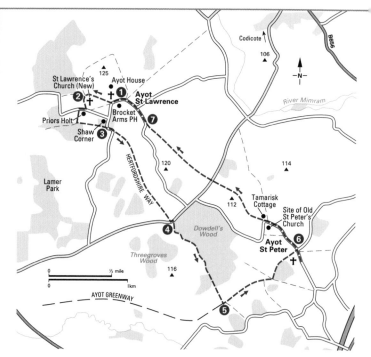

WELWYN GARDEN CITY Ebenezer's Vision

A walk around the first garden city.

4 miles/6.4km 2hrs **Ascent** 120ft/37m ⚠ **Difficulty** ☐1 **Paths** Town roads, parkland paths and woodland tracks, 2 stiles **Map** OS Explorer 182 St Albans & Hatfield **Grid ref** TL 235133
Parking Campus West Long Term car park (free on Sundays) off B195 in Welwyn Garden City

❶ Cross The Campus; pass **R** of department store, along Parkway. At 2nd traffic lights cross **R**, into Church Road. At its end turn **L** into Guessens Road, which curves **R**. Cross Handside Lane into Youngs Rise and then turn **L** into Elm Gardens. At end turn **R** into Applecroft Road.
❷ Turn **L** into The Links. Leaving Welwyn Garden City, go under A1(M) bridge and straight on into Lemsford, with River Lea to **L**.
❸ At Lemsford Mill turn **R** to cross river on stylish modern bridge. Follow footpath and bear **R** at junction, now on Lea Valley Walk. You are soon in Brocket Park, this part golf course. Carry straight on where **R-H** fence ends. Cross tarmac path to footpath post –thatched tennis pavilion is behind fence here.
❹ Turn **R** but follow drive for about 20 paces, then carry on across golf course, guided by waymarker posts. Footpath climbs **R**, out of dry valley and, passing cottage, you head out of Brocket Park. Go through kissing gate and turn **L** into Brickwall Close, with Waggoners pub on **R**. At Ayot Green turn **R** and cross A1(M).

❺ At T-junction turn **L** and almost immediately **R**, down to stile leading into woods. Go diagonally **L**, not sharp **R**. At bridleway junction bear **R**, path descending to cross course of old railway line. At Six Ways (carved totem poles) turn sharp **L** on to bridleway. Pass through car park to lane. Turn **R**, with parkland to Digswell Place on **L**.
❻ At Digswell Place Mews turn **R** by waymarker post, to return to woods. At bridleway post bear **R** uphill – path carries on straight through woods. Ignore all turns until you reach waymarked bridleway running off **R**. If you miss it, you soon come to houses and school. Follow bridleway as it bends **L** to houses and gardens. Pass alongside fences, eventually bearing **L** to merge with track and leave woods. Go straight over Reddings into Roundwood Drive and on to tarmac path between gardens.
❼ Turn **L** on old railway trackbed (Hatters Line), then **R** up fenced ramp, out of cutting and back to Campus West car park.

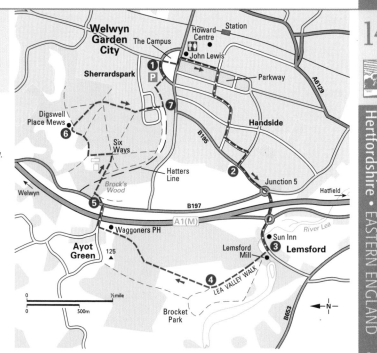

HARPENDEN In Rothamsted Park

A stroll through Rothamsted Park.

5.5 miles/8.8km 2hrs 30min **Ascent** 110ft/34m ⚠ **Difficulty** 2

Paths Field tracks, former railway line, pavements, 1 stile

Map OS Explorer 182 St Albans & Hatfield **Grid ref** TL 132140

Parking Amenbury Lane car park, Harpenden

❶ From Amenbury Lane car park, go **R**, into Hay Lane. Past Harpenden Leisure Centre enter park and follow path to lime avenue. Turn **R** and continue along avenue to T-junction.

❷ Turn **R** here into another lime avenue. After 4 trees go **R**, through gate at bridleway sign, and head diagonally **R** to gate in far corner.

❸ Turn **L** then **R** to join lane. When road turns **R** towards Rothamsted Experimental Farm go **L** on tarmac track and then **R** at bridleway sign, path now grassy margin. Continue across lane on to path between fields and follow it as it curves **L** down to Knott Wood. Walk alongside it and, out of field, turn **L** on to Nickey Line path.

❹ Path follows course of this former railway line to Harpenden Road. Cross road, skirt to **L** of roundabout and go up **R-H** side of A5183. Path regains trackbed. Just past gates to caravan site go **L** through gate to cross A5183.

❺ Over main road climb steps to gate. Continue across arable field, with electricity poles to **L**. Go through hedge gap and straight on, then bear **R**. Path goes into overgrown green lane, shortly with golf course to **L**. Pass behind 8th tee and turn **L** along golf course side of hedge. Past 9th tee turn **R**, path winding through scrub. Beyond this go through gate and some pasture, bypassing Hammonds End Farm.

❻ Turn **L** along lane then **R** on to Redbourn Lane. At White Horse pub go **L** by Flowton Green, then turn **R** on to footpath to **L** of Flowton Grove. Beyond thatched cottage you reach road along west side of Harpenden Common.

❼ Turn **L** and walk past Rothamsted Research. Continue alongside West Common into Harpenden. Go along High Street to Church Green and parish church. From here walk south to Leyton Green. Finally turn **R** into Amenbury Road and car park.

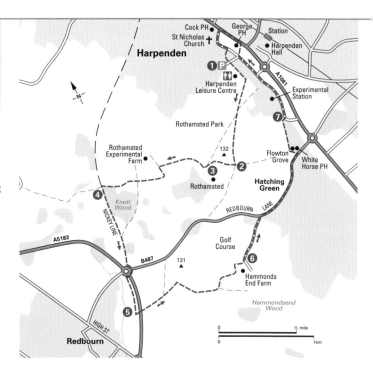

GREAT GADDESDEN A Rich Parish

A walk within the parish of Great Gaddesden.

6 miles/9.7km 3hrs **Ascent** 240ft/73m ⚠ **Difficulty** 2
Paths Field paths and bridleways, 13 stiles
Map OS Explorer 182 St Albans & Hatfield **Grid ref** TL 030137
Parking The Green, Jockey End

❶ From The Green go past bus shelter and turn **L** at footpath sign into paddocks. Walk alongside hedge. Where it ends cross to hedge. Turn **L**, then pass through oak and thorn scrub to road.

❷ Cross road on to Bunkers House drive, bearing **L** at its gates. Walk alongside garden hedge, then cross cultivated field. Go through hedge and turn **L**.

❸ Cross stile by large oak, then head diagonally to **R** of The Hoo, house in remnants of 18th-century parkland. Follow fence towards woods, then enter them. From woods descend across arable land to hedge, following field edge as it curves **R** to road by houses.

❹ Cross into water-meadows. Walk across footbridge, then bear **L** towards parish church. Beyond Victorian, brick and flint school, turn **R** to enter churchyard.

❺ From southwest corner of churchyard, cross pasture to road. Turn **R**, then go **L** at footpath sign by cottages. In field, head to gate, go through it and follow grass margin to arable land. Turn **R** at crest. At footpath T-junction turn **L** to head for woods. Once in them walk ahead for few paces, then turn **L**, path descending to valley. At gate bear **R** to footbridge and then go between buildings to road.

❻ Go through 2 gates beside cottages, climb stile, and turn **L**, uphill, across cultivated land towards porticoed Gaddesden Place. Go into parkland, pass through 2 gates, and head uphill, to **L** of oak and then to waymarker post to **L** of mansion.

❼ Past Gaddesden Place and through field gate, head to trough. Bear **R** to gate, avoiding Chiltern Way running **L**. Cross fields. Turn **L** on to track to Home Farm. At wood edge go **R** at footpath sign to walk beside wood.

❽ Path then enters ancient lime avenue. Leave this at valley bottom by turning **L** on to track. At track junction go **R** and immediately diagonally **L** towards gate, passing sweet chestnuts, to another gate.

❾ Once through this, continue through sequence of paddocks and stiles, passing The Lane House, crossing road and continuing northwest, passing copse. Beyond copse you reach road, turn **R** here, back to Jockey End.

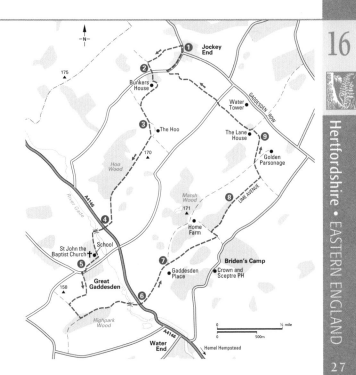

TRING Delights And Surprises
From Tring up into the Chilterns and back through Tring Park.

5.5 miles/8.8km 2hrs 30min **Ascent** 335ft/102m ⚠ **Difficulty** 2
Paths Pavements, footpaths, 1 stile
Map OS Explorer 181 Chiltern Hills North **Grid ref** SP 925114
Parking Car park at east end of Tring High Street (except market day, Friday)

❶ Walk along High Street, past church; turn **L** at crossroads down Akeman Street to Natural History Museum at Tring. At Park Street turn **R**, then go **L**, up Hastoe Lane, to leave Tring under A41 bypass.
❷ Just beyond bridge turn **R** at footpath sign, 'Stubbing's Wood'. Beyond A41 cutting, at gate and stile, bear **L** to climb ridge, with hedge on **L**. Reach Stubbing's Wood; follow its edge, then enter it, keeping **L**. At path fork bear **R** – route is marked by arrows on trees. Keep **R** at fork. Pass footpath sign, 'Shire Lane Pavis Wood', then descend to sunken way and turn **L** along it. Climb towards gateway and out of woodland. Continue along metalled lane. At junction turn **L**, briefly on to Ridgeway National Trail along Gadmore Lane. Leaving Trail at crossroads, turn **R** on to Browns Lane, metalled bridleway.
❸ Turn **L** at footpath crossroads on to Chiltern Way. Follow Grim's Ditch. Keep **R** at fork. After about 1.25 miles (2km) on Chiltern Way go through kissing gate on to Chesham Road.

❹ Turn **R** at road, then **L** through kissing gate, still on Chiltern Way. At lane turn **L**; at electricity sub-station turn **R**. Chiltern Way veers **R** but here leave it, instead following **L-H** hedge, to hedge gap and waymarker post. Cross dry valley – church belfry is visible opposite. At hedge line head diagonally **L** into cattle pasture. Through kissing gate turn **R** on to Chesham Road and proceed to Wigginton Church.
❺ From church head north along Twist, winding downhill to Ridgeway National Trail signs. Turn **L** to follow trail to just beyond cottages (Ladderstile and Westwood). Go straight on, into woods of Tring Park.
❻ At cross path where Ridgeway turns **L**, turn **R** to Temple, or Summer Pavilion. Head west to Obelisk. Still in woodland, continue downhill to kissing gate. Bear **R** here, into superb cattle-grazed, 18th-century parkland, to head for footbridge over A41. Across bridge follow footpath back into Tring – route is clear, near town being mainly between high walls – emerging in High Street.

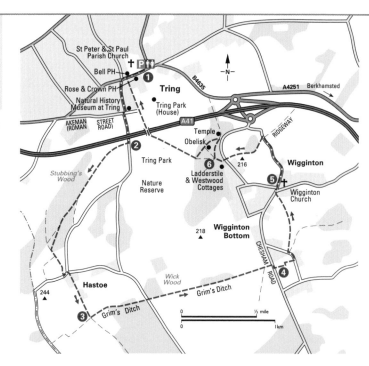

ASHRIDGE PARK A Wedding Cake

A walk in Ashridge Park and wooded commons of Chiltern plateau.

6.5 miles/10.4km 3hrs **Ascent** 225ft/69m ⚠ **Difficulty** ☐2
Paths Mostly tracks through woodland or parkland
Map OS Explorer 181 Chiltern Hills North **Grid ref** SP 976128
Parking Car park on Aldbury Common, on road to Bridgewater Monument

❶ From car park on Aldbury Common head towards distinctive column of Bridgewater Monument, turning **L** at footpath sign. Keep straight on along track until, just before pond, go **L** by footpath post at track crossroads.
❷ At road, cross on to bridleway. Woodland gives way on **L** to parkland with cattle grazing. Track bears **R** into woodland, skirting paddock and Woodyard Cottages, to reach metalled track. Follow it to **R**, still within woodland. At footpath crossroads, before gate to farm buildings, go **L** on to track. At track fork bear **L** and, reaching field, follow path that descends along **R-H** edge of woods to tree belt then runs through it to road.
❸ Turn **L** on road and, past ornate Berkhamstead Lodge, bear **R** at footpath sign, to climb through woodland. At crest walk alongside wire fencing and grounds of Ashridge College.
❹ Cross drive at side of college and walk across football field between 2 sets of goal posts, looking for yellow waymark by trees. Route crosses Prince's Riding here, with vista terminated by Bridgewater Monument.

Continue through copse and follow more white posts. Cross dry valley and then golf practice range. Beyond practice tees path winds through copse to road.
❺ Turn **R** along road, now Chiltern Way. Where it turns **L**, footpath bears **R** between garden hedges, across fairway, then between gardens and past gate to Witches Hollow. At footpath crossroads turn **L** on to metalled track.
❻ Follow metalled lane downhill. Past drive to Witchcraft Hill it becomes path through woods. Over stile path bears **L** alongside clearing, then into woods to road at Ringshall.
❼ Turn **L** here and cross main road. Follow verge and pass gardens, turn **R** into woodland of Ivinghoe Common. At National Trust bridleway post bear **L**, then **L** again to walk along ride, ignoring turns **L** and **R**. Eventually cross dry valley and, at bridleway post where track bears **R**, go almost straight on to wind through wood to Prince's Riding and car park.

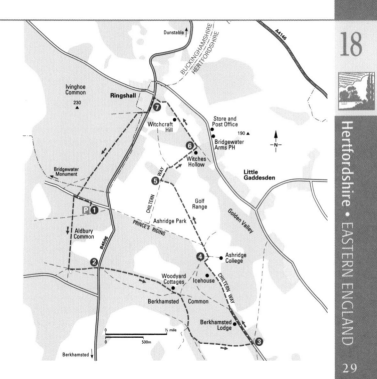

LONG MARSTON Advancing On The Tring Salient

A walk on lowlands of the Vale of Aylesbury around Long Marston and Puttenham.

4 miles/6.4km 2hrs **Ascent** Negligible ⚠ **Difficulty** ☐

Paths Field paths alongside hedges, some roads, canal tow path, 8 stiles

Map OS Explorer 181 Chiltern Hills North **Grid ref** SP 898156

Parking Along village roads in Long Marston

❶ From crossroads by Queen's Head pub walk north along Station Road which curves past Boot pub. Continue past war memorial to visit Victorian Church – All Saints. Return to war memorial. Now turn **R**, down Chapel Lane, towards medieval tower of old church, set amid trees beyond thatched Old Church Cottage.

❷ Opposite, go through 5-bar gate and walk diagonally across field to stile. Cross track and climb another stile to walk along **R-H** side of stream and hedge through several fields. Head for tower of Puttenham church in distance, using it as directional landmark. Over footbridge, turn **R** to another one and, over this, walk across pasture to Puttenham church.

❸ Follow lane, past Cecilia Hall, to road junction. Turn **R** to walk along road, but, where it turns **L**, carry straight on, past Rectory Stables. At modern farm cottages go **L** over stile by footpath sign to follow hedge south then west, around 2 sides of field. Over stile and through another field, next hedge and stile is

Buckinghamshire county boundary. Crossing another path, path passes alongside corrugated iron sheds. At track, head for canal bridge beyond its 10-ton limit signs.

❹ Go over bridge No 8, then descend **L** to canal tow path; follow this through bridge No 7, past 2 locks, to bridge No 5.

❺ Leave tow path and cross bridge No 5. Bear **R** to follow **L-H** side of hedge and stream. Follow path through several fields, then cross lane and head north along green lane, ignoring stile to **L**. Shortly, climb stile to follow overgrown lane beside stream. Emerging from scrub, cross corner of field, leaving it via gate to **L** of electricity pole. Path crosses arable field to footbridge. 2 more stiles bring you to lane (Astrope Lane) and public footpath sign, 'Wilstone 1 mile'. Turn **R** to walk back to crossroads in Long Marston.

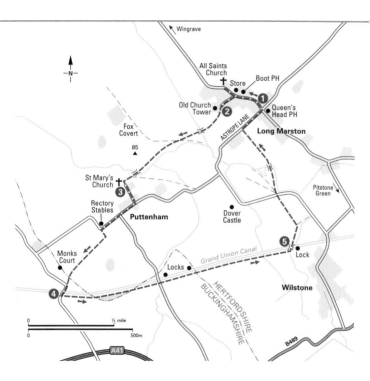

ALDBURY Transport Arteries

Across the railway to the Grand Union Canal and the woods of Aldbury Nowers.

5 miles/8km 2hrs **Ascent** 230ft/70m ⚠ **Difficulty** ⬜1
Paths Bridleways, field paths, canal tow path, woods, 1 stile
Map OS Explorer 181 Chiltern Hills North **Grid ref** SP 965124
Parking Around green in centre of Aldbury or in public car park up Stocks Road at north end of village

❶ From village green, visit St John the Baptist Church. Leave via lychgate. Turn **R** to kissing gate, signposted 'Pitstone Hill', and turn **R** on to Hertfordshire Way. Past farm buildings and across track, path climbs gently between hedge and fence. At crest turn **L** on to bridleway, with golf course on **R**. Drop to join Ridgeway National Trail, which reaches road via drive to Westland Farm.

❷ Follow road **R**, cross Northfield Road junction and then railway in its cutting. Passing Tring Station and former Royal Hotel and cottages, on **R** of bridge descend steps to Grand Union Canal tow path.

❸ This canal bridge is No 135. Follow tow path beside canal in its cutting as far as next bridge, un-numbered Marshcroft Bridge; climb up to lane.

❹ Turn **R** on to lane to Marsh Croft Farm. Go across railway and through gate on to concrete road. Pass Park Hill Farm, then horse paddocks. At road turn **L** and pass gates to Northfield Studio and copse. Turn **R**

beyond, to footpath sign set back from road, 'Pitstone and Pitstone Hill'. Go through gate on to path skirting old chalk pits. Go across footpath junction to climb steeply alongside woodland, with downland **L**, to reach Pitstone Hill.

❺ Turn **R** through kissing gate into woods of Aldbury Nowers, following Ridgeway. Here path follows section of Grim's Ditch along ridge until, descending, you veer **L** down steps. Ignore turnings off. At footpath T-junction, where Ridgeway turns **R**, go **L**. At guidepost go straight on, initially in woods, ignoring path to **R**.

❻ Go through kissing gate and across track. Path, now on golf course, curves downhill through trees, then turns **L** at hedge. At sign go **R** and keep on metalled track, with hedge **R**. At next hedge go through kissing gate, path now between high hedges.

❼ Turn **L** on to bridleway to road. Turn **R** to follow Stocks Road back to Aldbury village.

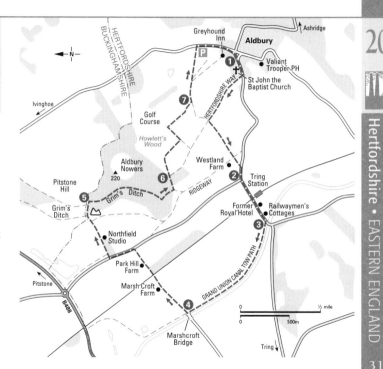

21

HARROLD ODELL Working Up An Appetite

Enjoy a day out at a country park.

4 miles/6.4km 2hrs **Ascent** 197ft/60m ⚠ **Difficulty** 2
Paths Park tracks, field-edges and woodland paths, 3 stiles
Map OS Explorer 208 Bedford & St Neots **Grid ref** SP 956566
Parking Country park car park, near Harrold

① Leave car park by visitor centre and walk to far end of park beyond main lake – either along semi-surfaced path between 2 lakes or across long meadow by side of River Great Ouse (difficult after heavy rain). Go through gate at far end of main track and along lane to pub at Odell, with its riverside garden. Beyond this join pavement of High Street on rising bend and cross over at top, before reaching church.

② Go through double gate on **L** for public bridleway– not footpath further on beside church. Follow wide grassy track uphill between fields, ignoring paths and tracks off **L** and **R**; follow this broad, direct route into Odell Great Wood. After 0.25 mile (400m) of woodland walking reach major junction of routes.

③ Turn 1st **L**, almost back on yourself, for public footpath (indicated on nearby waymarked post) through trees to southwestern edge of wood. Turn **L** and walk along perimeter to end, then don't go through inviting hedge gap, but turn **R** through metal gate to follow field edge to far corner.

④ Turn **L** and go over high stile to follow series of field edges gradually downhill to road at bottom – and admire pleasant views over the country park and river valley as you do so. St Nicholas's Church, isolated on a hilltop on the far side of the river, is particularly prominent, and a little to the west is the 14th-century tower of St Peter's Church at Harrold. The final field is a narrow, enclosed grassy strip used by local stables.

⑤ Cross road and turn **L** to walk along pavement. In 150yds (137m) go **R**, down through wide field opening, and follow **R-H** side of field as it zig-zags around to far corner.

⑥ Re-enter country park and turn **R** on to semi-surfaced path that skirts northern side of main lake. At far end either walk along grassy strip back to visitor centre or follow path into woodland by road, and turn **L** for short and shady track back to start.

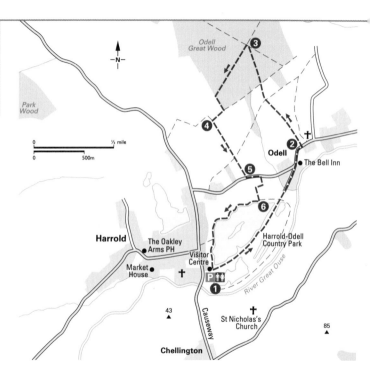

Bedfordshire • EASTERN ENGLAND

32

ROCKINGHAM FOREST Flying Kites

An ancient forest, now home to red kites.

5 miles/8km 2hrs 30min **Ascent** 426ft/130m ⚠ **Difficulty** 2
Paths Firm forest tracks, woodland and field paths, 8 stiles
Map OS Explorers 224 Corby, Kettering & Wellingborough or 234 Rutland Water **Grid ref** SP 979982
Parking Forestry Commission car park, Fineshade Wood (off A43)

1 With Top Lodge visitor centre and café on **L**, walk along lane past Forestry Commission's offices, and fork **L** where track divides. After passing houses, it soon becomes wide, semi-surfaced forest drive.

2 Just before you reach 2 semi-detached cottages (Nos 2 and 4 Top Lodge), detour for broad gravel track on **L** that leads through trees to wildlife hide (free) overlooking artificial pond and open ground. Continue along main track through open woodland until, just after 1 mile (1.6km) from start, turn **R** at crossroads of paths, indicated 'Jurassic Way'.

3 Take this track through trees, with field opening up to **L**. When field ends, go straight over junction of paths into Westhay Wood and, in few paces, join main forest track to continue south through woodland.

4 At junction at very far end, where main track turns abruptly **R**, go **L** and walk through small timber yard to Wood Lane. Walk to old railway bridge.

5 To visit village of King's Cliffe continue to bottom of lane, cross and turn **L** – pub and church are at far end of West Street. Otherwise turn **R** before railway cutting for field edge footpath. At border of Westhay Wood continue through fields alongside woodland, until in far corner path disappears into trees.

6 Follow well-waymarked route (direction arrows attached to some trees), which at one point crosses former railway by remains of old footbridge. Follow old fence; eventually emerge into fields. Walk around **R-H** edge, beside trees, until clear path cuts across corner to woodland on far side.

7 Continue along path through conifers, then turn **R** on to wide farm track that drops down, via gate, on to open hillside above Fineshade Abbey (private).

8 Turn **R** along fenced path above buildings and on across tree-covered hillside. Go over wide and dipping field; turn **R** on to lane at far side to car park at top.

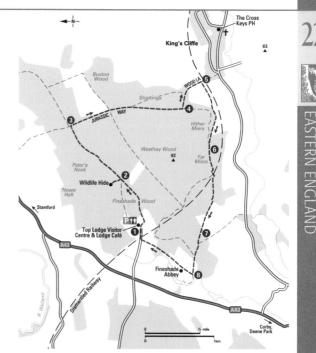

CASTLE ASHBY A Fine State Of Affairs

A varied walk that takes in a leisurely river and a grandiose mansion.

6.5 miles/10.4km 3hrs **Ascent** 557ft/170m ⚠ **Difficulty** 2
Paths Field paths, farm tracks and river bank, some steps
Map OS Explorer 207 Newport Pagnell & Northampton South **Grid ref** SP 859594
Parking Roadside in Castle Ashby, or car park for visitors

❶ Walk out of Castle Ashby heading southwestwards, with house (and visitors' car park) over to **L**. Where pavement ends turn **R** for Chadstone. Drop down lane past cottages and expensive-looking converted barns to farm of Chadstone Lodge.

❷ Turn **L** for bridleway behind hedge and, at end, go on through trees to continue the route alongside next field and down to road. Cross over for footpath down to Whiston Spinney, then via footbridge in dell to reach junction of tracks on far side. Here go straight on, and climb directly up sloping field ahead to trees on far side.

❸ Follow path into woods to climb steps and head out along field edge with woodland on **R**. Beyond gate go down sharp flight of steps to **R** and across field; turn **L** on far side and drop down to road below.

❹ Route continues up through field opposite. Head half **L**, then follow bridleway waymarks to **R**, through long narrow field with houses of Cogenhoe on **L**. At far

side join lane and descend to Cogenhoe Mill.

❺ Just before old mill buildings and sluice, with holiday park beyond, turn **R** for path alongside River Nene (signposted 'Nene Way'). Follow this waterside walk for 1 mile (1.6km) as far as Whiston Lock, then turn **R** for straight farm track across fields to main road, heading towards Whiston church sitting astride hilltop like lighthouse.

❻ Go across junction and walk along lane into Whiston, branching **L** at small triangular village green. Take gated passageway beside outbuildings of Manor Farm up to church. There are good views across the Nene Valley to Earls Barton and Wellingborough, and the eastern edge of Northampton.

❼ Walk past church to far side of churchyard; go over metal rung in wall and turn **R** on to obvious field edge path. This continues along grassy strip between fields and emerges on to bend of lane. Go straight on **L** to walk back to Castle Ashby.

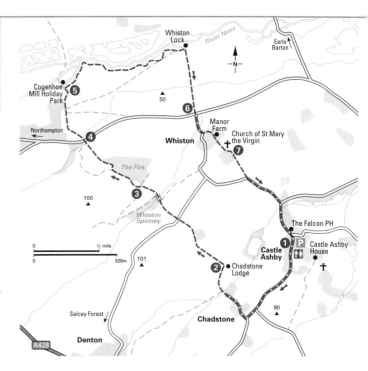

BADBY A Village Trail

Three lovely villages west of Northampton.

6.75 miles/10.9km 3hrs 30min **Ascent** 787ft/240m ⚠ **Difficulty** ③
Paths Mostly pasture, muddy where cows congregate, 11 stiles
Map OS Explorer 207 Newport Pagnell & Northampton South **Grid ref** SP 559589
Parking On Main Street, Badby

❶ With your back to The Windmill at Badby, walk up Vicarage Hill to reach Badby church. Take alleyway path signposted 'Fawsley', opposite south side of church, then head **R** up sloping field for path around western edge of Badby Wood, famous for its springtime bluebells.

❷ After about 0.25 mile (400m) take **R** fork (upper path), and follow waymarks for Knightley Way out across open hilltop of Fawsley Park and down towards lakes near hall.

❸ Go ahead along lane at bottom to inspect church, otherwise turn **L**, and in few paces **L** again (before cattle grid) for footpath that heads up and across large sloping field. Go through gate and down track to road, then resume opposite climbing steadily through fields, passing Westcombe Farm on **L**. Continue across Everdon Hill and down to Everdon below, joining lane via stile to **R** as you near bottom of hill.

❹ Walk through village, following road as it bends **L** past church and pub, and turn **L** for lane to reach Little Everdon. When road appears to split go ahead/**L** for path to **L** of farm buildings. This continues out across open fields, with Everdon Hall **R**. On far side, pass end of strip of trees and maintain northwesterly direction to carry on through 4 more fields and reach river (aim just **R** of Newnham's church spire when it comes into view).

❺ Cross Nene via footbridge and walk uphill through 1 field, then veer **L** in 2nd to cross 3rd, and drop down to pick up farm drive which, beyond gate, becomes Manor Lane. Walk on to join main street.

❻ Turn **L** and drop down past pub by The Green and continue along Badby Road out of village. In 150yds (137m) go **L** for field-edge paths alongside infant River Nene.

❼ Cross footbridge at end and walk half **L** through field ahead, keeping **L** of trees in middle and aiming for Badby church. At far corner turn **R** into Chapel Lane to return to centre of Badby.

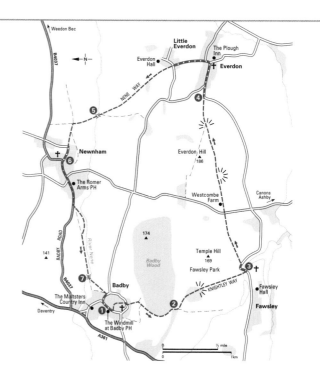

OUNDLE The Banks Of The Nene
A riverside meander around Oundle.

6.75 miles/10.9km 3hrs **Ascent** 115ft/35m ⚠ **Difficulty** 2
Paths Waterside meadows and farmland tracks, 4 stiles
Map OS Explorer 227 Peterborough **Grid ref** TL 042881
Parking Oundle town centre (long-stay car park off East Road)

❶ From end of Market Place, in centre of Oundle, walk down St Osyths Lane, then South Road until it curves **R**, then go straight on into Bassett Ford Road. Where this bends **L** into Riverside Close go ahead to gate at end. There are 2 riverside walks indicated – make sure to go half **L** across field and follow bank downstream (not over footbridge ahead).

❷ For next 2.25 miles (3.6km) route follows bank of Nene as it completes giant loop. Go underneath Oundle bypass and eventually out by open meadows.

❸ Eventually, beyond weir, you reach long, high footbridge where can cross river for visit to picturesque village of Ashton, round trip of 0.75 mile (1.2km). Otherwise continue ahead and back under bypass to reach old bridge.

❹ Cross over road and turn **R** across bridge. On far side of river turn **L** at Riverside Walk sign, past boat sheds, and strike out along flat eastern bank of Nene via 2 weirs. Take path around 2nd weir and cross footbridge to continue along riverside path.

❺ Cross river via so-called 'guillotine' lock and continue to lane at far end by converted corn mill. Turn **L** and walk through pretty Cotterstock, and after 550yds (503m) turn **L** before red telephone box for narrow path between fence and hedge.

❻ This heads out along **L-H** side of open field, then beside narrow plantation with river on far side. Continue past sewage works and directly down through 2 more fields before reaching playing field.

❼ Half-way along pitch turn **L** for hedge gap and boardwalk out to Nene – this is permissive route through Snipe Meadow nature reserve. Turn **R** and walk along river bank until just before bridge, then head **R** for Oundle Wharf. Go through field beside buildings to reach New Road.

❽ Turn **L** to end of road, then **R** into Station Road/North Street to town centre.

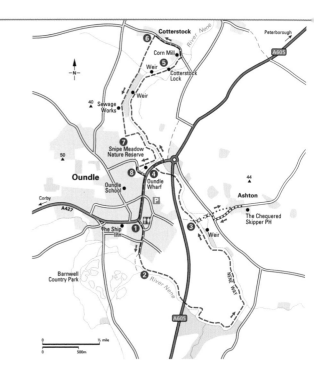

WICKEN FEN The Last Survivor

A walk through an authentic fen.

4.75 miles/7.7km 2hrs **Ascent** Negligible ⚠ **Difficulty** 1
Paths Mostly river banks and farm tracks, potentially slippery
Map OS Explorer 226 Ely & Newmarket **Grid ref** TL 564706
Parking Wicken Fen nature reserve car park (pay-and-display) if visiting the reserve, otherwise off Wicken High Street

❶ From car park walk up Lode Lane towards Wicken. Before you meet main road turn **R** on to Back Lane and follow this, which soon becomes pleasant track running behind houses. At far end of lane, just after windmill, turn **R** on to wide track through fields. (If you have parked in village centre take signposted public footpath via Cross Green, just along from and opposite pub, out to fields.)

❷ Follow this wide route down to 2 footbridges. Cross 2nd bridge and turn **R** along bank of Monk's Lode, with St Edmund's Fen opposite.

❸ After 550yds (503m) branch **L** before fence and gate for long straight track (drove); head across fields to Priory Farm. Join surfaced lane and continue to end.

❹ Turn **R** by raised Cockup Bridge and walk along bank of Burwell Lode (don't be tempted by footbridge). Continue for 1.5 miles (2.4km) past Adventurers' Fen, named after 17th-century 'Gentlemen Adventurers' who first started draining the fens in earnest.

❺ At high-arched footbridge over Wicken Lode turn **R** and walk along bank back towards Wicken Fen past National Trust sign. If you continue across footbridge and walk for another 0.25 mile (400m) you come to Upware, with pub and picnic area. Ignoring paths off into open fen and fields on **R**, continue along bank until its junction with Monk's Lode. Across water you pass lofty thatched Tower Hide.

❻ Cross short bridge by Goba Moorings and continue alongside Wicken Lode, not along Monk's Lode (to **R**). Lush vegetation of Wicken Fen is now either side.

❼ When you get to end turn **L** to visitor centre (open daily from Easter to October, Tuesday to Sunday in winter). There is small admission charge to reserve itself, which is open daily from dawn to dusk. Near by is restored Fen Cottage, and lovely thatched boathouse where reserve's traditional working fen boat is kept. To return to car park and village, simply walk back up lane past houses.

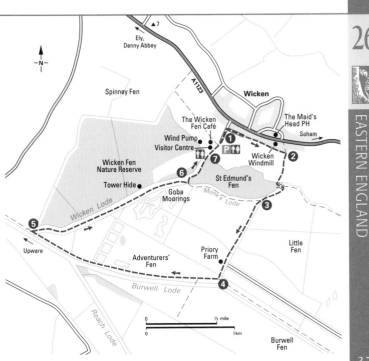

MANEA Fenland's Big Skies

An enigmatic landscape links remote Manea with an historic drainage cut.

6.25 miles/10.1km 3hrs **Ascent** Negligible ⚠ **Difficulty** 2
Paths Lanes and hard farm tracks, field-edge paths, 1 stile
Map OS Explorer 228 March & Ely **Grid ref** TL 478893
Parking Roadside parking in centre of Manea

1 With Rose & Crown pub on **L**, walk eastwards along Manea High Street and follow it round to **L** as it becomes Station Road, then turn **R** for public footpath alongside primary school. At football pitch at far end turn **R** and go past Manea Wood, planted in 1997 for local community with ash, oak, white willow, birch and common alder. Continue along path as it bears **R** and approaches Bearts Farm.

2 Turn **L** by old barns and sheds for wide track out into fields, and bear **R** at junction of tracks to reach attractive reedy lake known locally as 'the Pit'. This was originally dug for clay, which was then transported across the fields on a light railway to shore up the banks of the nearby Old and New Bedford Rivers. The Pit is now a popular place for fishermen and wildlife alike.

3 At end of track turn **R** on to lane, with lake still on **R**, then, when you reach junction at corner of road, turn **L**, on to Straight Road, and follow this through fields to end.

4 Turn **L** on to Purls Bridge Drove, signposted 'Welches Dam' and 'RSPB reserve'. Follow this open lane to Purls Bridge, by Old Bedford River. Continue along bank to reach Ouse Washes Nature Reserve (visitor centre and public toilets).

5 Return along lane for 440yds (402m) and turn **L** for signposted public bridleway by dark wooden sheds. Known as Old Mill Drove, this runs directly across open fields as far as rusting farm machinery and outbuildings of Boon's Farm. Turn **R** and walk along dead-straight Barnes's Drove for 1.25 miles (2km) to road at far end.

6 Turn **L** and after 150yds (137m) turn off **R** through gate for public footpath across fields back into Manea. The route zig-zags between series of paddocks – just follow clear yellow waymarks and aim for fire station tower. At far side cross stile and turn **R**, past village stores, to follow main road back to centre.

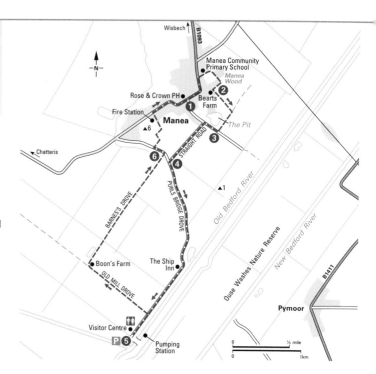

EXTON The Miniature Charm Of Rutland

Explore the open countryside and parkland around Exton.

6.5 miles/10.4km 3hrs **Ascent** 425ft/130m ⚠ **Difficulty** 2
Paths Mainly field paths and firm farm tracks, 10 stiles
Map OS Explorer 234 Rutland Water **Grid ref** SK 924112
Parking Roadside parking on The Green, Exton

1 With your back to pub leave The Green on far **R-H** side on Stamford Road and, at end, turn **R**. This becomes Empingham Road and, when houses finish, continue over stream and go over stile on **L** to follow public footpath.

2 Just before gate at entrance to field, bear **R** to follow wide, grassy track along shallow valley, keeping stream to **R**. Stay on track for just under 1 mile (1.6km), at one point crossing stream and returning via footbridge before climbing into field on **L** to avoid Cuckoo Farm. Finally path crosses stream again and clambers up through fields on **R** to reach lane.

3 Turn **L** and walk along verge until just beyond bend, then go **L** on footpath indicated 'Fort Henry and Greetham'. Follow this route above trout hatchery, then head diagonally **R** via small concrete bridge to fence at top. Turn **L** and walk along to Lower Lake, then go ahead on surfaced drive for few paces, to fork **L** before gate and head out across open pasture above water.

4 At far side turn **R** on to another lane then, in few paces, **L** for footpath indicated 'Greetham'. Follow this beside Fort Henry Lake, then on along corridor between mixed woodland. At far end climb stairs to reach lane.

5 Turn **L** and walk up through more woods and, when semi-surfaced drive bears **L**, go straight on through newly planted trees. Wide, unmade track now heads directly out across open fields for 1 mile (1.6km).

6 At trees on far side turn **L** on to track that drops down and bears **L**. Here go straight on via stile and wooden plank footbridge and head up diagonally **L** towards top of field. Go over stile and turn L on to farm track once more.

7 At junction turn **R** on to straight, metalled lane, 'Viking Way to Exton'. Bear **L** at fork before woods and follow this back to Exton. Follow signs around Home Farm, then follow West End round to **L** and turn **R** by stone shelter into High Street to return to The Green.

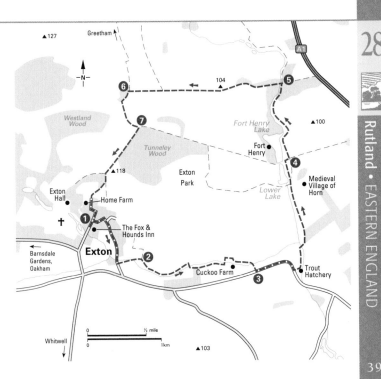

RUTLAND WATER A Waterside Walk

A short but scenic introduction to the aquatic charms of Rutland Water.

4.5 miles/7.2km 2hrs **Ascent** 311ft/95m ⚠ **Difficulty** 1
Paths Wide and firm the whole distance, 3 stiles
Map OS Explorer 234 Rutland Water **Grid ref** SK 900075
Parking Roadside parking in Hambleton

❶ From St Andrew's Church in centre of Hambleton, walk east on long main street as far as red pillar box. Turn **L** opposite pillar box on wide track indicated 'public footpath' that leads straight through gate and down middle of sloping field.

❷ Go through gate at bottom of field and turn **R** on to wide track that runs just above shore. This popular and peaceful route around the Hambleton peninsula is shared with cyclists, so enjoy the walk, but be alert. Follow it from field to field, and through Armley Wood, with ever-changing views across Rutland Water. As you gradually swing around the tip of the Hambleton peninsula with views towards the dam at the eastern end, you can begin to appreciate the sheer size of the reservoir, and how the birds, anglers, sailors and other users can all happily co-exist.

❸ When you reach tarmac lane (gated to traffic at this point, since it simply disappears into water further on!), go straight across to continue on same unmade

track. It turns **R** and runs parallel with road short distance, before heading **L** and back towards peaceful water's edge and section of mixed woodland. Continue along lakeside for just over 1 mile (1.6km).

❹ Approaching The Old Hall turn **L** to reach its surfaced drive, then go **R** and walk along it for 160yds (146m) to reach cattle grid.

❺ Now you can return to Hambleton by following lane back uphill; otherwise veer **L** to continue along open, waterside track, with views across to Egleton Bay and corner of Rutland Water specially reserved for wildlife (out of bounds to sailing boats).

❻ After about 500yds (457m) look for easily missed stile in hedge on **R**, and public footpath straight up field. (If you overshoot, or to extend walk by 0.5 mile/800m, carry on along track to far end and return along lane to village.) Aim for apex of field, where stiles lead to narrow passageway between hedge and fence that eventually brings you out in churchyard in village.

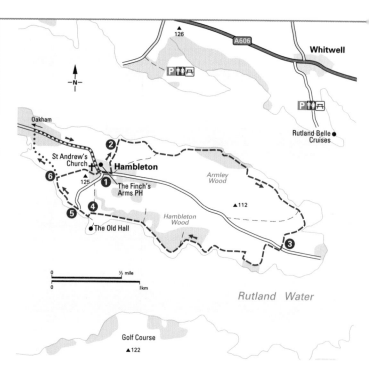

FRISBY ON THE WREAKE A Village Ramble

Wander through the Wreake Valley.

3.75 miles/6km 1hr 45min **Ascent** 150ft/40m ⚠ **Difficulty** ☐2
Paths Pasture, ploughed fields heavy if wet, 14 stiles
Map OS Explorer 246 Loughborough **Grid ref** SK 694176
Parking Roadside parking on Main Street or Water Street, Frisby

❶ Walk east along Main Street, past post office, and turn **L** into Mill Lane. After 50yds (46m) turn **R** between houses on public footpath (denoted by fingerpost bearing footprint). Walk out across open field, dropping slightly downhill, then go through double gate and ahead through 2nd field.
❷ Ignore turning down to railway (**L**), but instead continue across wide fields, with Ash Tree Farm away to **R**. Despite lack of well-walked path route is clearly indicated by yellow-topped signposts, until you reach road.
❸ Go across and continue through 2 smaller fields, 2nd in which horses are usually kept, and via kissing gate in corner to reach houses of Kirby Bellars. Turn **L** and walk down lane to church.
❹ Continue down narrowing lane, which twists **L**, then **R**, past nursery. Track emerges into open field; turn **L** and follow clear path across meadow. Go over stile by lifebuoy for leafy path along causeway across Priory Water, former gravel pits now run as nature

reserve. At end go ahead over more stiles, as path veers **L** and follows bank of River Wreake. It then winds through copse to end at road bridge into Asfordby.
❺ To visit Asfordby turn **R** and take surfaced pathway off to **R** on far side of bridge. Otherwise cross road (but not bridge) for path opposite, which initially shadows river then strikes out diagonally L across 2 fields. Aim for far corner of 2nd, with spire of Frisby church just in view above treetops ahead.
❻ Turn **R** and walk along narrow, grassy field parallel with railway, then negotiate railway via pedestrian crossing. Follow lane on far side until it bends **L**. Here go **R** into Carrfields Lane, then **L** via short alleyway and another quiet back street to reach Church Lane. Turn **L** and follow this back to Main Street. Entrance to church is via side of old school building.

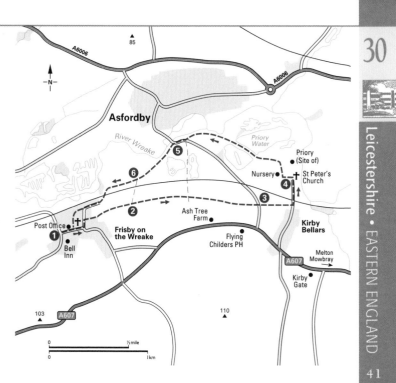

MEDBOURNE Curious Customs

Unusual Eastertide goings-on in two villages.

7.5 miles/12.1km 4hrs **Ascent** 787ft/240m **⚠ Difficulty** 3

Paths Farm paths, tracks, some rough and muddy, 15 stiles

Map OS Explorer233 Leicester & Hinckley (224 Corby, Kettering & Wellingborough, also useful)

Grid ref SP 799929 **Parking** Roadside parking near village hall, Main Street, Medbourne

❶ Walk up Main Street and turn **R** on to Rectory Lane, opposite church, which becomes path. Go over road at end and up through fields opposite. Cross stile to continue through yard of Nut Bush and across field beyond, then climb over low wall on **L** to road. Turn **R** and walk along road to Nevill Holt.

❷ Turn **L** at end and, where brick wall finishes go **L** through gate to cross wide arable field. Go through gate and drop down through 2 fields, separated by Uppingham Road. Beyond woodland strip go **L**, then up **R-H** side and across top of next field– aim for solitary tree on skyline. At far corner drop down to **R** to join track. Turn **R** at junction and walk on farm track into Blaston.

❸ At Church of St Giles turn **L** and follow Hallaton Road to junction at end. Go straight over and after 2nd stile turn **R** to walk through open pasture towards Hallaton. Follow yellow-topped waymark posts, aiming initially for spire of Hallaton church, then veer to **R** of trees in middle of field, and cross footbridge.

❹ Go **L**, then sharply **R** beyond stile and follow signs through small housing development. Eventually turn **L** on to Medbourne Road and straight on to centre of Hallaton.

❺ Leave village via passageway underneath house, just along from Bewicke Arms and almost opposite Butter Cross. Cross footbridge and go directly up sloping field, aiming just **R** of wooden fence beneath trees. Arriving at summit of Hare Pie Bank, go through gate and turn **L** on to wide track (Macmillan Way). Continue along edge of 2 gated fields, then turn **L** into lane. Turn **R** at 1st bend and follow this long, semi-surfaced lane below Slawston Hill.

❻ At road junction go straight over and down lane, and 500yds (457m) beyond former railway bridge turn **L** for unswerving bridleway along foot of successive fields. At far end, turn **L** to follow road back into Medbourne.

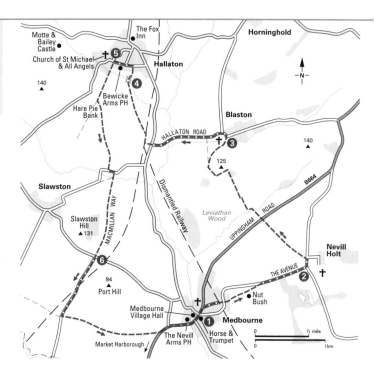

FOXTON LOCKS Flights Of Fancy

Discover a staircase of locks.

5 miles/8km 2hrs 30min **Ascent** 213ft/65m ⚠ **Difficulty** 2

Paths Canal tow path and open fields (mostly pasture), 6 stiles
Map OS Explorer 223 Northampton & Market Harborough **Grid ref** SP 691891
Parking Foxton Locks long stay car park (pay-and-display)

❶ Turn **L** out of car park and go along signposted path parallel with road to canal. Go **R**, under road bridge, then over footbridge, to turn **R** on far bank and along tow path to Foxton Locks. Descend lock staircase to reach basin at bottom.

❷ Go ahead past Bridge 61 pub and switch banks via high-arched brick footbridge (Rainbow Bridge). Walk out along wide tow path beyond. Continue along this easy and peaceful route for 1.75 miles (2.8km), following Grand Union Canal as it swings **L** beyond Debdale Wharf. Notice large numbers of boats moored in the marina, some in preparation for repairs and renovation, while others are kept here permanently. There are lovely views over the open countryside towards Kibworth Beauchamp to the north.

❸ At bridge No 68 cross stile on **R** to cross metal footbridge via 2 more stiles. On far side make your way up **L-H** edge of wide, sloping field to pass Debdale Grange. Continue alongside top field to reach lane on far side.

❹ Turn **R**, along road for 0.25 mile (400m), then, approaching road junction, go over stile on **L** for a signposted public footpath across field. Take **R** fork, aiming for far edge of Gumley Wood – **L-H** signposted 'Foxton' takes you back to canal. Follow path closely around side of plantation until 2nd stile, beside section of fence used as horse jump.

❺ From here strike out across undulating grassy field towards metal gate below trees on far side. Aim half **L** through next field. Go through another gate and directly out across more fields, separated by farm drive, to return to canal on far side. Cross high, thin footbridge and turn **R** to return to basin and locks. Walk back up beside staircase, crossing over half-way up to visit museum.

❻ From museum follow popular path up along its side (don't cross main canal again), then briefly double back to **L** along canal arm through trees. Cross bridge and turn **R** along tow path to return to road bridge. Go under this and turn **L** to return to car park.

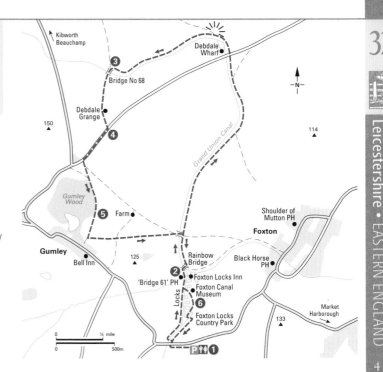

33

MARKET BOSWORTH Doing Battle
Visit England's most famous battlefield site.

8.25 miles/13.2km 4hrs **Ascent** 279ft/85m ⚠ **Difficulty** ③ **Paths** Easy lanes and tow path, may be muddy, 8 stiles **Map** OS Explorers 232 Nuneaton & Tamworth; 233 Leicester & Hinckley
Grid ref SK 412031 (on Explorer 232)
Parking Market Bosworth Country Park (pay-and-display)

❶ Walk down wide track from car park to reach playground and adjoining spinney, and continue across wildflower meadow to woods beyond. Follow main gravel path through trees and bear **L** at a fork. Look for wide kissing gate on **L**.

❷ Go through and follow path for 0.5 mile (800m) along edge of woodland and past Looking Glass Pond.

❸ Go over stile and on past **R** of Woodhouse Farm. Path continues down along **L-H** field edge, then crosses stream to climb **R-H** side of next field.

❹ As hedge falls away well-walked path heads out across middle of field before turning **R** approaching (but not quite at) top. It keeps to top of next field, then turns **L** across another to reach car park of Royal Arms Hotel. Turn **R** and walk through Sutton Cheney until, just past church entrance, you turn **R** at road junction (signposted 'Shenton').

❺ Follow lane as it forks **L** and in 550yds (503m) turn off **L** through Cheney Lane car park and follow clearly marked path across fields to heritage centre.

❻ Walk past heritage centre below car park and continue across picnic area to junction of paths. Turn **R** and follow waymarked Battle Trail across Ambion Hill to reach Shenton Station. Cross railway line by gate and turn **L** out of car park entrance on to lane. Walk along as far as canal bridge.

❼ Go over bridge to double back and turn **L** beneath bridge on to towpath of Ashby Canal, signposted 'Market Bosworth'.

❽ After 2.5 miles (4km) of towpath walking, leave canal at King's Bridge (No 43), one after Bosworth Wharf Bridge. Cross this, then railway bridge for field-edge path across stiles. Path heads half **R** across golf course – aim **L** of house in front of hilltop woodland. Cross stile and go along top of field before joining unmade lane which takes you into Market Bosworth.

❾ At end join narrowing road (Back Lane), **L** and ahead, that comes out in Market Place. Cross over and walk past The Old Black Horse Inn, then turn **L** into Rectory Lane. At end of lane is country park.

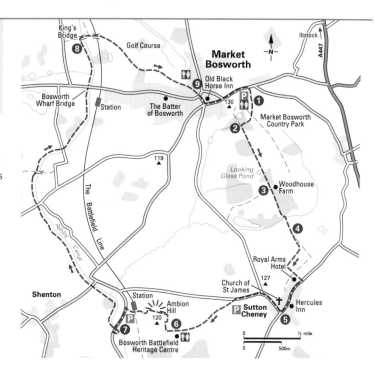

Leicestershire • EASTERN ENGLAND

44

BRADGATE PARK Among The Deer

In Leicester's scenic Bradgate Country Park.

3.75 miles/6km 1hr 45min **Ascent** 558ft/170m ⚠ **Difficulty** 2
Paths Easy surfaced tracks and undulating paths, 2 stiles
Map OS Explorer 246 Loughborough **Grid ref** SK 522098
Parking Car park at Newtown Linford (pay-and-display)

1 Enter grounds from car park at and turn sharply **L** on wide track. Go through open gateway and, ignoring paths off **R**, stick on main route uphill (there are in fact 2 parallel tracks), keeping park's boundary wall in sight on **L**.

2 When you draw level with large wooden swing gate in wall, fork **R**. Go steadily uphill on wide grassy ride through banks of bracken, past small plantation known as Tyburn, and soon you will see prominent hilltop war memorial up ahead on **L**. Follow obvious grassy track to 'summit', then go round to **R** of walled plantation behind to reach folly known as Old John Tower. Although centre of Leicester is only 6 miles (9.7km) away, views from this viewpoint (695ft/212m) are predominantly rural, with large tracts of woodland.

3 Turn **R**, straight down hillside, to small circular pond in bracken below. Take **L** of 3 paths on far side and continue to track around walled plantation known as Sliding Stone Enclosure. Turn **L** and walk along this track for 100yds (91m).

4 Ignore path straight down to gate in wall on 3, and instead go straight on. Grassy track drops down to park's boundary wall, then continues uphill on short tarmac strip past small underground reservoir.

5 After 125yds (114m) take track off **R**, by wooden bench and, rather incongruously, 2 drainage covers. Long, straight grassy track heads across middle of country park and is easy to follow. It passes between Coppice Plantation and Dale Spinney, from where there are good views across Cropston Reservoir. Continue down to reach surfaced drive at bottom and turn **R** to visitor centre (open April to October).

6 Continue along this easy, tarmac route past ruins of Bradgate House and restored chapel, then on alongside pools and waterfalls of small valley known as Little Matlock. Look out for monkey puzzle tree and cedar of Lebanon, introduced to park in the 19th century. Continue back to car park.

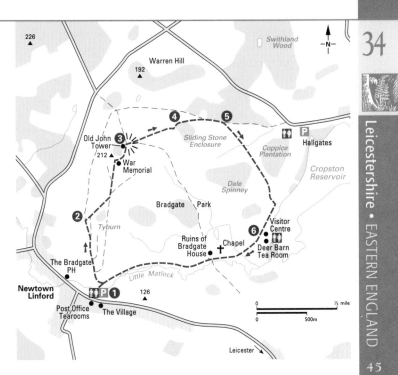

WEST LEAKE HILLS Panoramic Hills

An enjoyable walk with great views.

4.25 miles/6.8km 2hrs **Ascent** 246ft/75m ⚠ **Difficulty** ②
Paths Field-edge paths, farm lanes and forest tracks, 3 stiles **Map** OS Explorer 246 Loughborough
Grid ref SK 527264 **Parking** Roadside parking near West Leake church

❶ Walk across road from church, half-way along West Leake's main street, to cross stile opposite. Go between houses and across open field. Go over stile at far side and turn **R** to follow field-edge path to end.

❷ Go through to next field and turn **L**. Now follow clear route alongside hedge, past vegetation-choked pond (often dry in summer), and out across middle of subsequent fields on obvious farm track. Far away to **L** are massive cooling towers of Ratcliffe-on-Soar power station.

❸ When you arrive at wide gravel track, turn **R** and follow this to edge of woods, marked by yellow-topped public bridleway sign and notice warning you to go no further.

❹ Go **L** before hedge and after 275yds (251m) turn **R** for bridleway route (waymarked with blue arrows) up steep hillside between trees. At top this becomes clear, straight path through attractive mixed woodland of Leake New Wood. On far side go through gate and cross to far side of field.

❺ At junction of bridlepaths, go through gate and turn **R** to walk along initially open hilltop, with expansive views to **L** over Trent Valley towards Gotham and distant Nottingham. Continue along this easy, panoramic route via Court Hill for almost 1 mile (1.6km). Beyond trees of Shiddock's Spinney golf course appears on **L**. At fork of paths keep **R** to end up alongside arable field on **R** and not fairway on **L**.

❻ At Crow Wood Hill reach bend of semi-surfaced lane. Turn **R** and follow its southwesterly route across open fields of Fox Hill, with wide views over to red-tile roofs of East Leake.

❼ When drive turns into Fox Hill Farm go straight on along clear field-edge track ahead, and ignoring path off to **L**, follow this long, straight route back down to West Leake. The vista now stretches out southwards, where the wooded ridges of Charnwood Forest (especially Beacon Hill and Bradgate Park) dominate the skyline. At road junction at bottom go straight on for centre of village.

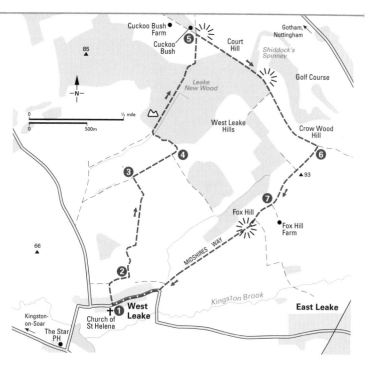

LAMBLEY Deep In The Dumbles
The hidden dells of Lambley's Dumbles.

6.25 miles/10.1km 3hrs **Ascent** 508ft/155m ⚠ **Difficulty** ③
Paths Undulating paths and green lanes, over 20 stiles
Map OS Explorer 260 Nottingham **Grid ref** SK 627452
Parking Recreation ground car park behind school (opposite The Lambley, on Catfoot Lane)

❶ From The Lambley pub, walk down Main Street into village centre. In 220yds (210m) go **R** for public footpath between houses and around edge of fenced field. Turn **L** at end and cross successive stiles (at 2nd take **L-H** choice) for path behind houses. Turn **L** at end to drop down, cross road, and enter Reed Pond Nature Reserve.

❷ Veer **L** to gate in far **L** corner. Turn **R** and out along bottom of several large fields, cutting across lower part of 2nd. Continue around edge of copse and with large sloping field ahead turn **L**.

❸ Follow wide track uphill to **L** of hedge. In far corner of 3rd field, with grassy airstrip along its middle, turn **L** (not footpath straight on) and walk along field edge.

❹ Just before it ends go **R** and, following direction of footpath post (not bridleway), aim half **L** across next field then bear **L** across pasture. Drop down hillside, aiming for stile beyond wooden enclosure in far corner by road.

❺ Turn **R** and walk along roadside verge past Woodbarn Farm to sharp **R-H** bend. Go **L** across top of successive fields to wooded track on far side. Turn **L** and stay on this path as it bends **L** and becomes wide trail back to junction with Lingwood Lane.

❻ Turn **R**, cross field (aiming half **L**), then follow waymarks down through 3 fields into woodland at bottom. Go straight on via footbridge, **L** into field on far side, then almost immediately **R** and walk up through field to top. Climb steps and turn **L** on to road for 100yds (91m), then go **R** beside bungalow to drop down diagonally **R** across ridged fields to football pitch.

❼ At far corner continue on popular (and obvious) path to walk through newly planted woodland area known as Bonney Doles. Cross footbridge, turn **L**, and follow field edge to corner.

❽ Here short path with handrail ventures into bumpy wooded dell. Ignore this and continue around to cross another footbridge. Turn **L** and follow path through woods, then field bottom along south side of Lambley Dumble, eventually turning **L** on to Spring Lane to return to car park.

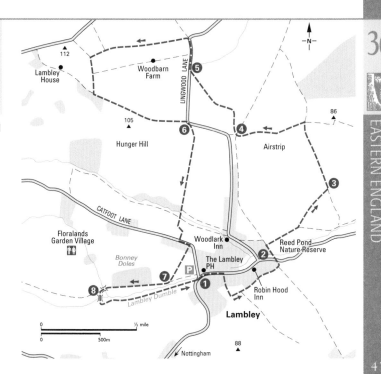

EASTWOOD In The Footsteps of D H Lawrence

Explore the countryside that provided inspiration for much of the writer's work.

5.75 miles/9.2km 2hrs 30min **Ascent** 360ft/110m **⚠ Difficulty** **2**
Paths Rough field and woodland tracks, 2 stiles **Map** OS Explorer 260 Nottingham
Grid ref SK 481481 **Parking** Colliers Wood car park, Engine Lane, off B600

1 Walk out of entrance of Colliers Wood car park and turn **R**, then **L** along pavement of B600. At bend turn **R** by Beauvale Lodge and take track to its **L** (signposted 'Felley Mill'). Walk this pleasant fenced route through High Park Wood, above Moorgreen Reservoir, branching L after 0.25 mile (400m) just before gate. Carry on along main track until open field appears on **R**.

2 Continue walking for another 150yds (137m), then turn **R** at stile and walk up **L-H** side of patchy line of trees separating 2 fields. At far side turn **L** and follow woodland edge. Go around corner and, joining wide farm track, continue alongside forest. (Site of Felley Mill is away to **L** at foot of slope.) After 0.5 mile (800m) turn **R** beyond bench to locate public footpath through trees.

3 Where this emerges at junction of 3 forest rides go straight ahead. With growl of nearby M1 motorway getting louder, turn **L** after bend on to clearly indicated footpath into woods. This emerges to follow field edge, swinging **R** on far side and eventually reaching lay-by.

4 Turn **R** if you want to view remains of Beauvale

Priory, otherwise go **L** and walk down lane to bend by intriguingly named 'Brook Breasting Farm'. Go sharply **R**, along **L-H** field edge, then turn **L** and drop down through 2 more fields. Look for gap in undergrowth to **R**, and go over footbridge.

5 Turn **L** and follow direction of sign across lower part of field. Continue along top edge of successive fields, going **R** to skirt final sloping field before dropping down to road.

6 Cross over and turn **R** to enter churchyard of St Mary's at Greasley. Walk around church and exit churchyard at far side on footpath signposted 'Moorgreen'. After crossing cemetery, go across field and continue to walk alongside paddocks to reach road at top.

7 Turn **L** and almost immediately **R** for enclosed path between houses. Follow waymarks across and down through fields, and at bottom go **R** for path back into Colliers Wood. Turn first **L** to reach ponds; beyond is car park.

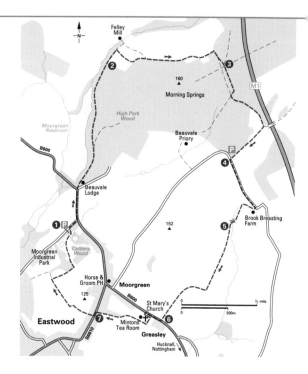

Nottinghamshire •
EASTERN ENGLAND

NEWSTEAD ABBEY Byron's Romantic Home

Explore Byron's beautiful mansion.

5.75 miles/9.2km 2hrs 30min **Ascent** 460ft/140m ▲ **Difficulty** ☐1☐
Paths Firm, uncomplicated paths and tracks, 1 stile
Map OS Explorer 270 Sherwood Forest **Grid ref** SK 541540
Parking Newstead Abbey car park, access from A60 (note closing times)

❶ From main car park walk down drive to abbey, then on along tarmac lane below large Upper Lake. Follow this easy route for 1.25 miles (2km) until you leave perimeter of park after 2nd lodge.

❷ Immediately turn **L** and cross stile to reach small, dumpy hill adorned with young trees (Freckland Wood). Airy and quite easy path runs up and across panoramic top, or else you can skirt **R-H** foot on waymarked National Cycle Network Route 6. Both routes meet up on far corner for direct 1.25-mile (2km) track to Linby.

❸ Turn **L** when you emerge close to roundabout, and walk along pavement through village to Horse & Groom pub. Cross over; continue eastwards out of village on pavement opposite 2nd of 2 medieval road-side crosses.

❹ When **L-H** pavement ends cross again and take popular local footpath across Church Plantation. Continue across River Leen, then halfway up next field go through archway in hedge on **L** to reach tiny Church of St James. Leave churchyard, via main gate, and proceed down surfaced drive to main road. Turn **L** and

walk along pavement for 550yds (503m) until entrance for Papplewick Hall.

❺ Turn **L**, not to enter hall's gated driveway but for wide, semi-surfaced Hall Lane that runs via green gate past Top Farm. Where lane bends sharply **L**, around prominent brick wall, go straight on, via gate, along hedged farm track across fields. Where farm track turns **R** to Newstead Grange, go straight on along main grassy track towards wooded park perimeter.

❻ Follow waymarks around lodge and continue along surfaced drive through trees – look out for ancient beech and oak along way. About 0.75 mile (1.2km) beyond lodge, lane bends **L** and path branches off ahead/**R**, clearly indicated. Soon it drops down to reach main drive to abbey.

❼ Turn **L** and walk along road to the car park and abbey for some well-earned refreshments, and perhaps a spot of poetry.

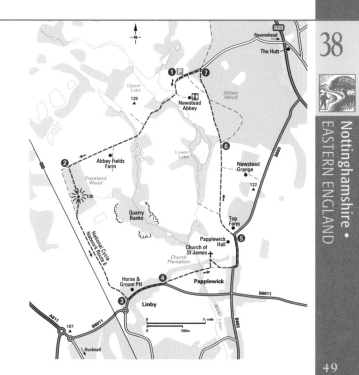

SHERWOOD FOREST A Merrie Tale

Walk among the oaks of this legendary forest.

5.5 miles/8.8km 2hrs 30min **Ascent** 278ft/85m ⚠ **Difficulty** 1
Paths Easy woodland tracks and wide forest rides **Map** OS Explorer 270 Sherwood Forest
Grid ref SK 626676 **Parking** Sherwood Forest Visitor Centre (pay-and-display)

❶ Facing main entrance to Visitor Centre from car park, turn **L** and follow well-signposted route to Major Oak.

❷ Go along curving path as it completes semi-circle around impressive old tree and continue as far as junction with public bridleway (signposted). Turn **L** here, then walk this straight and uncomplicated route for 0.25 mile (400m), ignoring paths off.

❸ At green notice board, warning of nearby military training area, main path bears **L**. Instead go straight ahead, past metal bar gate, for path that continues over crossroads to become wide, fenced track through pleasant open country of heather and bracken known as Budby South Forest.

❹ At far side go through gate and turn **L** on to unmade lane, walk this route for 0.75 mile (1.2km).

❺ At major junction just before plantation begins, turn **L**, indicated 'Centre Tree'. With rows of conifers on **R**, and good views across Budby South Forest on **L**, keep to this straight and obvious track. Where track divides into 2 parallel trails, gravelly track on **R** is technically

cycle route, while more leafy and grassy ride to **L** is bridleway, but either can be used.

❻ When you reach Centre Tree – huge spreading oak – 2 routes converge to continue past bench down wide avenue among trees. Don't go down this, but instead turn **L** and, ignoring paths off **R** and **L**, carry straight on along main track back into heart of forest.

❼ After almost 0.75 mile (1.2km) you pass metal bar gate on **R** and then meet bridleway coming in from **L**. Ignoring inviting path straight ahead (which returns to the Major Oak) bear **R** on main track, past bare holes and dips hollowed out by children's bikes. At large junction of criss-crossing routes go straight on (signposted 'Fairground') so that open field and distant housing becomes visible **R**. This wide sandy track descends to field by Edwinstowe cricket ground. The Art and Craft Centre and Sherwood Youth Hostel are on far side, and village centre beyond.

❽ To return to visitor centre and car park, follow well-walked, signposted track back up past cricket ground.

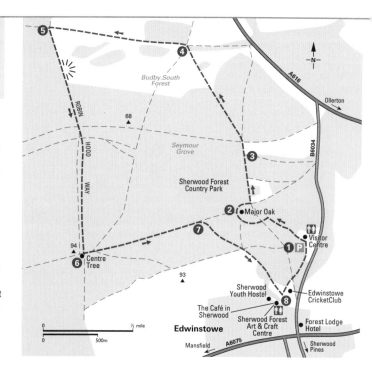

CLUMBER PARK Enjoying Country Life

Clumber Park provides an enjoyable day out for all ages.

3.75 miles/6km 1hr 30min **Ascent** 131ft/40m ⚠ **Difficulty** ①
Paths Clear, level paths and tracks throughout, some steps
Map OS Explorer 270 Sherwood Forest **Grid ref** SK 625745
Parking Main car park in Clumber Park (pay-and-display)

❶ From information point near main car park, walk across site of former mansion and down to reach lakeside. Turn **R** here along clear path that runs along shore through area of patchy woodland. Continue to follow path, which curves **L**, then **R**, to Clumber Bridge.

❷ Cross bridge and turn **L** past car park to resume route by shore. If path by water's edge below trees is little boggy, then switch to wider and firmer track further back. As you draw opposite site of former house, paths run across parkland to **R** – map is available from NT shop. At far corner of lake eventually swing **L** on embankment path. To **R** you'll find wetland area created 20 years ago by mining subsidence, now popular for birding. Carry on past toilet block at Hardwick to reach surfaced road beyond car park.

❸ Go **L** on to road and in 50yds (46m) turn **R**, before causeway begins, for narrow, sandy path up through dense vegetation. Follow this twisting route through area known as The Lings. The huge variety of trees here includes beech, sweet chestnut, silver birch, yew and pines. When you drop down and emerge into open, flat area beyond end of lake, walk ahead to turn **L** on to wide, curving gravel track.

❹ In few paces, where this narrowing route veers **L** towards shore, go straight on along **L** of 2 grassy paths. At end turn **L** on to wide track that crosses road and continues past wooden barrier into Ash Tree Hill Wood.

❺ Go straight over crossroads of tracks and on along this popular and direct route through trees, ignoring inviting **R** turn. Emerge in open ground on far side; continue ahead to ornate gateway into wooded Pleasure Ground ahead.

❻ Go through this, and veer **L** on any 1 of minor paths through undergrowth to main lakeside route. Turn **R** and follow this along Lincoln Terrace back to start of walk. A little beyond the lawned terrace looping track to **R**, across carefully manicured lawns, leads you to chapel and car park.

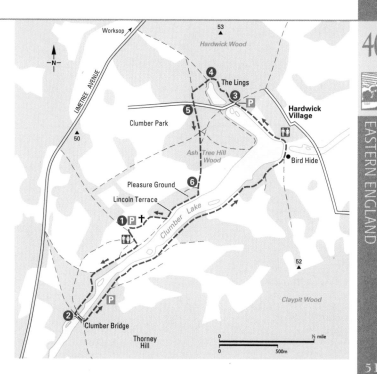

DANESHILL LAKES Wildlife Excursion

An easy stroll around a watery nature reserve near Retford.

3 miles/4.8km 1hr 30min **Ascent** Negligible ⚠ **Difficulty** ☐1
Paths Firm gravel tracks and woodland paths
Map OS Explorer 279 Doncaster **Grid ref** SK 668865
Parking Nature reserve car park, Daneshill Road, signed from A638

❶ From car park go through main gate and ahead past notice board on wide gravel track. At junction swing **R**, so that large lake opens up on **L**. Go past warden's office and sailing club hut along water's edge.

❷ Approaching railway look for 2 large trackside signs 'Edinburgh 250 miles'. 1st **L** turn is continuation of lakeside path, and 2nd **L** is via dog-run next to railway. Both join up 350yds (320m) later and resume easy tour around main lake. 2nd, smaller lake opens up on **R**.

❸ Meet fence at end, with open field beyond, turn **L**. As this bears **L** after 300yds (274m) take small grassy path into woods half **R**, beside notice board about former Ranskill Royal Ordnance Factory on this site. Now follow millennium wildlife trail indicated by wooden posts bearing letters 'MM'. It wanders happily through bushes and trees and beside small stream (look out for pond-dipping platform), and when it finally emerges from undergrowth turn **R** to return to car park. Continue via small path through trees to **L** of

road entrance and cross road.

❹ Go through gateway on opposite side and turn **L** on to narrow path, indicated 'Easy Access to Reserve' (ignore wide grassy footpath to **R**). Follow this track to reach wooden footbridge. Cross, then turn **R** and walk along to reach notice board by woodland pond.

❺ Continue to follow this easy and obvious track through reserve, keeping ditch and stream on **R** and ignoring inviting turning to **R** across footbridge.

❻ Unless you want to make diversion at this point to visit Ranskill as well, ignore **R** turn for Millennium Pathway, and instead stick to main path as it completes giant loop around entire nature reserve. Look out for shallow pools and scrapes among undergrowth, which, unless they've dried out in hot weather, are focus for creatures such as frogs and beetles. After about 1 mile (1.6km) or so you arrive back at wooden footbridge. Turn **R** here to cross it, go through gateway to road and cross over to car park.

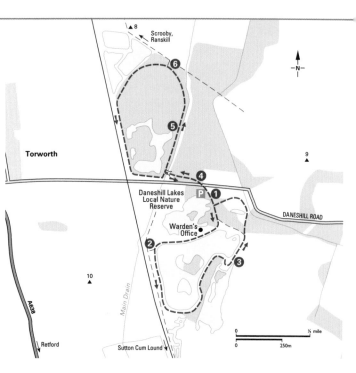

WOOLSTHORPE BY BELVOIR King Of The Castle
A fairy-tale castle and a lost canal.

4.75 miles/7.7km 2hrs **Ascent** 230ft/70m ⚠ **Difficulty** 2
Paths Tow path, field and woodland tracks and country lane, 2 stiles
Map OS Explorer 247 Grantham **Grid ref** SK 837342
Parking Main Street in Woolsthorpe by Belvoir

❶ Walk northwards out of Woolsthorpe by Belvoir on pavement of Sedgebrook Road, continuation of Main Street, towards Bottesford. Turn **R** into wide-verged lane for Rutland Arms public house (signposted) and cross over canal bridge at Woolsthorpe Wharf.

❷ Turn **L** and follow grassy bank along Grantham Canal until Stenwith Bridge (No 60). Climb steps to **R**, just before bridge, and turn **R** on to road. Follow this over old railway bridge and out along wide lane of oak trees. After 700yds (640m) it bends **L**, and here turn **R**.

❸ Follow initially hedged and unmade Longmoor Lane for just over 0.75 mile (1.2km). When you reach far end turn **L** before bridge, to join gravel tow path, and walk along this as far as elegant wooden arched bridge ('Bridle Bridge').

❹ Cross bridge and head out across middle of wide arable field. Go over course of old railway again and continue up **L-H** side of sloping field. At top, turn **L** on to well-walked track.

❺ Follow this pleasant route with lovely views out towards hills surrounding Grantham. Where track kinks **L**, after fenced section, go straight on **R** across wide field – follow direction of public footpath signpost and aim for hedge opening at very far side. Go across Cliff Road for track into woodland.

❻ At far side of woods, cross stile and turn **R** to follow field edge down bumpy, grassy slope back to Woolsthorpe. There are excellent views across head of Vale of Belvoir to Belvoir Castle opposite. At bottom of slope go over stile behind cricket scorebox, along edge of pitch (football ground to **L**), and down drive of pub to reach village centre.

❼ To extend walk to visit Belvoir Castle, turn **L** into Main Street, then **R** into Belvoir Lane. At end of this cul-de-sac cross small bridge and continue ahead across fields towards hilltop fortification. After 3rd stile, cross another stile to **R** and follow this wide track uphill to road, then turn **L** to castle entrance.

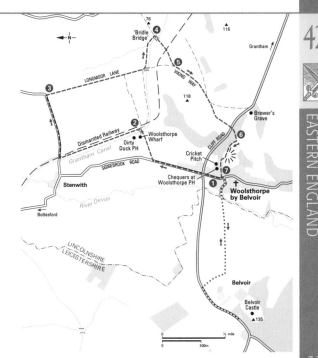

GEDNEY DROVE END Wildlife In The Wash

A wander on the South Lincolnshire coast.

5.75 miles/9.2km 2hrs 30min **Ascent** Negligible **⚠ Difficulty** 1 **Paths** Field-edges, firm tracks and sea banks, 1 stile **Map** OS Explorer 249 Spalding & Holbeach **Grid ref** TF 463292
Parking Roadside parking in centre of Gedney Drove End (off A17 east of Holbeach)

❶ With your back to The Rising Sun pub, turn **L** and walk along Dawsmere Road past junction and take signposted public footpath on **R**, between bungalows, opposite playground sign. At far side of field go across small footbridge and up steps to turn **L** into wide field.
❷ For 1 mile (1.6km) walk along field edge, which is in fact line of former sea wall, keeping more or less parallel with present and much higher sea bank over **R**. And as sign indicates, continue straight ahead at point where old sea bank veers invitingly away to **R**.
❸ When field eventually ends near strip of woodland turn **R** for 50yds (46m) then, faced with small thicket, drop down to join wide farm track on **L**. Turn **R**, and follow main, higher route (ignore lower track) alongside narrow shelter-belt of woodland which includes apple, cherry, hazel and birch. This wide, gravel track heads out towards sea bank then bends **L** and continues past Browns Farm.
❹ Stay on main track for about 0.75 mile (1.2km) beyond farm, then go **R** by old wartime pill box for

short path over to sea wall.
❺ Turn **R** and follow either grassy top of sea bank (public right of way) or surfaced lane just below it past succession of military observation towers. Bombing range is spread out before you, with Norfolk coast over to **R** and Lincolnshire seaboard towards Boston and Skegness **L**.
❻ After 3rd tower ignore gated road that heads off inland (short cut back to Gedney), but instead continue along sea bank past final watchtower until you reach stile. Cross stile and continue for another 400yds (366m).
❼ Turn **R** at public footpath sign, down steps, for direct path along field edge to junction of open lane. Here continue straight ahead into Gedney, turning **R** at end back on to Dawsmere Road. However, to prolong your Wash-side wander continue beyond stile for 1.25 miles (2km) until sea bank divides. Bend **R**, on inland arm, and join small lane before turning **R** on to Marsh Road back into Gedney Drove End.

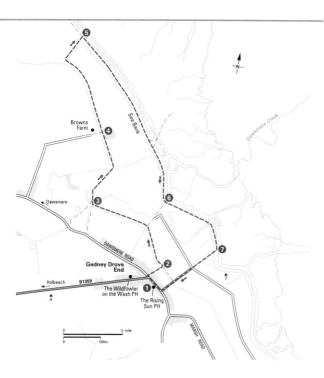

SALTFLEET On The Dunes

A wander along the wildlife-rich salt marshes of North Lincolnshire.

4.75 miles/7.7km 2hrs 30min **Ascent** Negligible ⚠ **Difficulty** 1

Paths Coastal tracks and field paths, some steps, 3 stiles
Map OS Explorer 283 Louth & Mablethorpe **Grid ref** TF 467917
Parking Nature reserve car park at Rimac, off corner of A1031

❶ Walk out of seaward end of car park and immediately turn **L** through gate, then climb steps to walk along top of dunes with sea away **R**. Go past Sea View farm and small parking area and continue beyond white barred gate, forking **R** to reach marshes. Go **L** and follow clear track along edge of marshes.
❷ At far end of dunes, join rough lane across 2 successive bridges, then turn **R** on to pavement of coast road. After 100yds (91m) cross another small bridge and turn **R** on to wide, bumpy lane indicated 'Saltfleet Haven'. Walk along this to small car park among dunes – bit further to view sandy bay and river mouth (tide permitting) where seabirds and sometimes seals can be spotted.
❸ At back of small car park, and with your back to Haven, go up steps and take 1 of several faint paths through dunes to pick up wide track that runs just seawards of vegetation-topped dunes (not along actual water's edge). Strip of marshes is spread out to **R**.

❹ In just under 0.5 mile (800m), turn **L** up concrete ramp by evergreen trees and walk down Sea Lane past caravan parks. Turn **L** at end, then **R** after Crown Inn into Pump Lane. At far end follow unmade track as it curves **L** between houses and, at hedge gap, take footbridge on **R** for path across fields.
❺ Crossing another footbridge to emerge on bend of Louth Road, turn **L** and, just after Hilltop Farm, turn **R**, across footbridge, for long field-edge public footpath.
❻ At junction of tracks at far side go straight on, over small stone bridge across ditch near house. Go over 1st of 3 wooden footbridges and continue alongside Mar Dike until you switch banks nearing far end to reach road.
❼ Turn **L** and walk down to crossroads. Go ahead and along drive opposite as far as Sea View farm. Turn **R** on waymarked public footpath through farmyard and field beyond, and continue on clear path along landward edge of dunes to return to car park.

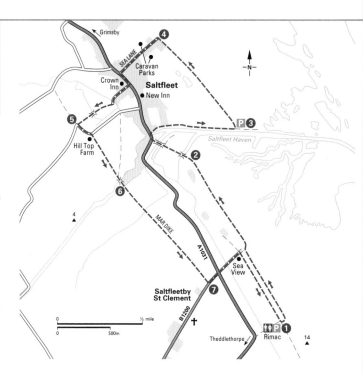

DONINGTON ON BAIN A Taste For Lincolnshire

A scenic walk through the Wolds.

6 miles/9.7km 3hrs **Ascent** 410ft/125m ⚠ **Difficulty** 2
Paths Bridleways and lanes, field paths, may be boggy, 10 stiles **Map** OS Explorer 282 Lincolnshire Wolds North **Grid ref** TF 236829 **Parking** Main Road, Donington on Bain

❶ Walk out of village northwards, past Norman church and post office, on to Mill Road. At 1st junction turn **R**, signposted 'Hallington' and 'Louth', then in few paces go **L**, over stile. Walk along bottom of successive fields, with River Bain on **L** and the lofty Belmont Transmitting Station dominating skyline further west. After 0.75 mile (1.2km), and having passed fishing lake, reach footbridge.

❷ Cross footbridge to reach Biscathorpe's isolated little church, rebuilt in the mid-1800s in a medieval Gothic style. Walk around its perimeter wall; continue past house and across lane to cross footbridge ahead.

❸ Now head half **L** across bumpy outline of deserted medieval village. Ditches, ridges and mounds give some indication of its layout. Head towards hilltop and go through gate for path through small plantation. Turn **R** on lane and walk along this for 550yds (503m).

❹ Go over stile on **R** for signposted public footpath down side of disused workings, then **L** across wide field, aiming for far corner down by stream. Go over

footbridge, then follow farm track round to **L** before crossing next footbridge and walking across meadow to lane at Gayton le Wold.

❺ Turn **R** and walk along lane past Manor Farm's whitewashed buildings and another miniature church, then out across hilltop fields. In 0.5 mile (800m), where lane bends **R**, go **L** on broad track indicated 'public bridleway'. Veer **R** into field at top and follow this obvious and waymarked route alongside huge ploughed fields. There are delightful views down across the Bain Valley to **R**, back towards Donington. Continue around and above back of Glebe Farm, by thick hedge, and go straight over lane.

❻ In just under 0.5 mile (800m) from road crossing, turn **R** where signpost points to public footpath downhill behind hedge. Follow this wide track gradually down via Horseshoe Plantations, then hedge by fields of grazing horses from stable near by. Turn **R** on to road at bottom to return centre of Donington on Bain.

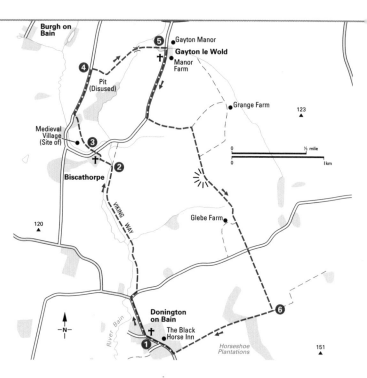

TEALBY Churches On The Wolds

A quiet ramble through two beautiful Lincolnshire villages.

4.25 miles/6.8km 2hrs **Ascent** 721ft/220m ⚠ **Difficulty** 2

Paths Field paths, some steep and others muddy
Map OS Explorer 282 Lincolnshire Wolds North **Grid ref** TF 157907
Parking Front Street, Tealby, near tea rooms

❶ From Tealby Tea Rooms walk down Front Street to B Leaning & Sons. Turn **R** into Church Lane, which soon becomes walkway. At top, turn **L** and cross Rasen Road to follow public footpath between houses on opposite side. As far as Walesby you will be following Norse helmet waymarks of Viking Way.
❷ Pass through gate and cross open pasture, aiming for another gate in far bottom corner. Go through and along path ahead, ignoring footbridge to **L**. Walk up open hillside ahead to reach corner of Bedlam Plantation which is above Castle Farm.
❸ Turn **R** and go through gate for fenced path beside woods. At far end head diagonally **L** down undulating grassy field to pass below Risby Manor Farm. Cross lane leading up to farmhouse and continue ahead, crossing deep valley and climbing steeply towards Walesby Top Wood. Pass through gate and keep ahead across field of crops to All Saints Church.
❹ Walk through churchyard and continue along Viking Way as it drops down wide track into village.

Reach Rasen Road at bottom; go straight on, past church of St Mary until you reach junction with Catskin Lane.
❺ Turn **L** and walk along Catskin Lane for 0.75 mile (1.2km). Just past **R-H** curve, turn **L** at entrance of farm drive and go over cattle grid. This is in fact public bridleway that leads back up to hilltop; but turn **R** in few paces and join footpath across rough pasture, initially parallel with road. Stay on path along **L-H** field edge to arrive at drive to Castle Farm.
❻ Public footpath now continues almost due east across vast sloping field beyond. At far side of field, pass through gate and drop down to cross wooden footbridge. Turn **R** on far side of bridge to rejoin earlier route back into Tealby, this time turning **L** up Rasen Road to visit All Saints Church. Drop down through churchyard and follow Beck Hill to memorial hall, then turn **R** along Front Street to return to start of walk.

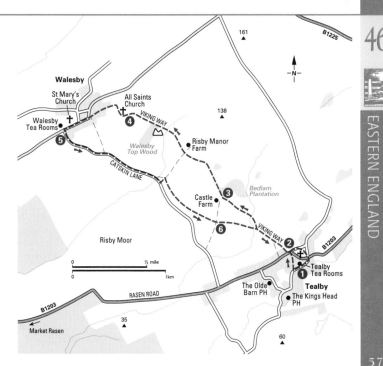

HARWICH Seafarers and Wanderers
An exciting maritime past.

4 miles/6.4km 1hr 30min **Ascent** Negligible ⚠ **Difficulty** 1
Paths Town streets and promenade with gentle cliffs
Map OS Explorer 197 Ipswich, Felixstowe & Harwich or 184 Colchester, Harwich & Clacton-on-Sea
Grid ref TM 259328 **Parking** Pay-and-display car parks at Ha'penny Pier and informal street parking

❶ With your back to Ha'penny Pier turn **L** along The Quay and follow road into King's Quay Street. Turn **L** just before mural, painted by the Harwich Society and Harwich School in 1982 and again in 1995, which depicts local buildings and ships. Follow road, with sea on **L**, until it turns inland. Take path by sea – start of Essex Way, a long distance path of 81 miles (130km) connecting Harwich with Epping. Pass Harwich Town Sailing Club and maintain direction along Esplanade where at low tide you can walk along shingle beach.
❷ Pass Treadwheel Crane on **R** and continue along seafront. Keep raised, fenced area of Beacon Hill Fort and gun emplacements to **R**. As you pass the breakwaters around bay there are views of Dovercourt. Ignore steps to **R**; continue along Essex Way, walking parallel with upper road of Marine Parade on **R**.
❸ Turn **R** into Lower Marine Parade and pass War Memorial and Gardens at junction with Fronk's Road and Marine Parade. Maintain direction passing Cliff

Hotel on **L** and then go **L** into Kingsway, opposite statue of Queen Victoria. Turn **R** into High Street and bear **L** into Main Road, passing police station on **L**. Walk for 250yds (229m) and turn **R** up track to see Redoubt Fort, Martello-style fort, part of defences against Napoleonic invasion. Continue to pass Cox's Pond, once owned by local bankers of the same name.
❹ Pass High Lighthouse on **R**, turn **R** into Wellington Road and **L** into Church Street passing St Nicholas' Church. Turn **R** into Market Street and **L** into King's Head Street, pausing to admire timber-framed houses including No 21, home of Captain Christopher Jones of the *Mayflower*.
❺ Turn **R** into The Quay, where Quayside Court faces sea. Now apartments, Quayside Court was built as one of the Great Eastern hotels in the 19th century and catered for travellers from the Continent who would arrive by steamer at what is now Trinity Quay and continue their journey to London by rail.

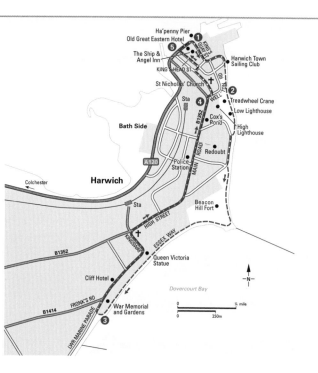

MANNINGTREE England's Smallest Town

Where the Witchfinder General was born and buried.

7 miles/11.3km 3hrs 30min **Ascent** 98ft/30m ⚠ **Difficulty** ☐2

Paths Field paths, footpaths, tracks and sections of road, may be boggy, 4 stiles

Map OS Explorer 184 Colchester, Harwich & Clacton-on-Sea **Grid ref** TM 093322

Parking Pay-and-display at Manningtree Station

❶ With your back to station turn **R** at public footpath sign to Flatford; after few steps turn **L** along steep, grassy path to St Mary's Church. Go through black gate and, church on **R**, cross stile over church wall. Turn **L** and, at wooden post, follow yellow waymark half **R** across meadow. Cross earth bridge over Wignell Brook; go **L** uphill. Keep line of trees **R** and go through kissing gate to join Essex Way. Just before house at top of hill, go through kissing gate and bear **L** to Cox's Hill, on to A137.

❷ Cross Cox's Hill with care, turn **L** and after 40yds (37m), at public footpath sign marking Essex Way, turn **R**. Walk downhill passing to **R** of pond and cross plank bridge over stream. Bear **R** to join gravel path through Owl's Flight Dell Conservation Area and pass to **R** of housing estate. Ignoring concrete path on **L**, turn half **R** on to cross-field path towards playing fields and join concrete path to road. Cross Colchester Road, and at T-junction turn **R** into Trinity Road, ignoring signs for Essex Way. At Evangelical church turn **L** between houses

to New Road. The Wagon at Mistley pub is on **L**.

❸ Cross New Road and follow yellow waymarked footpath between backs of houses. At T-junction turn **L** on to wide canopied bridleway. After 70yds (64m) follow waymark half **R** and rejoin Essex Way. Maintain direction, go through kissing gate, cross earth bridge over brook followed by stile and another kissing-gate. Keep ahead through thickly wooded slopes of Furze Hill. Emerge from woods; go ahead keeping to field-edge path to Church Farm. Turn **L** here on to Heath Road.

❹ Cross road to low wall to see remains of St Mary's Church. Continue north and turn **L** on to B1352 and into Shrublands Road which soon becomes green lane. Cross 1st stile on **R** towards EDME malt chimney and walk under railway. Keep ahead into The Green.

❺ Turn **L** into High Street, past Mistley Towers, and continue beside River Stour into Manningtree. Bear **L** along High Street and continue for 1 mile (1.6km) along Station Road to car park.

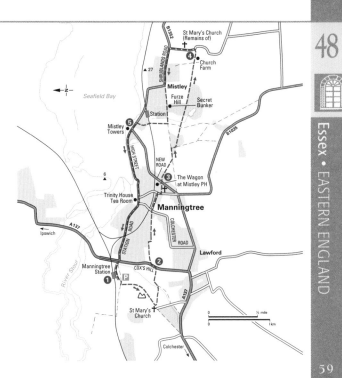

Essex • EASTERN ENGLAND

WALTON-ON-THE-NAZE Waltzing Around

A day beside the Essex coast exploring a town with two seasides.

4.25 miles/6.8km 2hrs **Ascent** Negligible ⚠ **Difficulty** 1
Paths Grassy cliff paths, tidal salt marsh and some town streets
Map OS Explorer 184 Colchester, Harwich & Clacton-on-Sea **Grid ref** TM 253218
Parking Pay-and-display at Mill Lane and Naze Tower

❶ From Mill Lane car park turn **R** into High Street then **L** into Martello Road. Bear **L** along New Pier Street and go on to Pier Approach. To **R** is Pier, its 0.5 mile (800m) length makes it 2nd longest in England, after Southend. From here there are good views of the beaches of Walton-on-the-Naze and Frinton.

❷ Turn **L** and, with sea **R**, walk along Princes Esplanade through East Terrace at end of which is the Maritime Museum. Continue walking along Cliff Parade and the cliff tops to Naze Tower. Built by Trinity House in 1720 as navigational aid, it was to join many Martello towers which were built along the east and south-east coasts to fend off Napoleonic invasion. Nowadays, grassy area in which tower stands is good place to rest and recuperate with hot drink and picnic at wooden tables.

❸ From car park café walk inland to Old Hall Lane, turn **L** and then **R** into Naze Park Road. At end of Naze Park Road, where it bears sharp **L**, turn **R** on to narrow path and **L** on to field-edge path passing 2 small ponds filled with wildlife.

❹ After 100yds (91m), turn **L** on to cross path, go through gate and on to permissive path which follows sea wall, keeping caravan site on **L** and Walton Channel on **R**. This wide expanse of mudflats, islands, channels and small boats, ever changing with the tide, is a paradise for seabirds and a Site of Special Scientific Interest (SSSI). Skippers Island, an Essex Wildlife Trust nature reserve, is the habitat of rare seabirds and wildlife and full-time wardens are employed to protect them. Follow sea wall for 0.75 mile (1.2km) then bear half **L** down embankment and into field used as overflow car park.

❺ With school field on **L** follow railings for 70yds (64m) to path between school and terraced cottages and continue to Saville Street past old cottages on **R**. Take 1st **R** into North Street, continue to High Street and turn **R**. Turn **R** again into Mill Lane to car park.

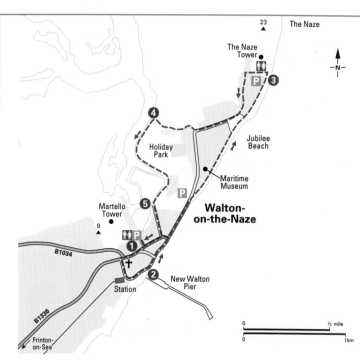

PAGLESHAM Paddling Up The Creek

A stroll along the sea wall.

6.25 miles/10.1km 2hrs 45min **Ascent** Negligible ⚠ **Difficulty** ☐2
Paths Grassy sea wall, field-edge, unmade tracks, 3 stiles
Map OS Explorer 176 Blackwater Estuary, Maldon **Grid ref** TQ 943922
Parking Informal street parking at Paglesham Eastend beside the Plough and Sail inn

❶ Walk to **L** of The Plough and Sail inn along driveable track, and after 100yds (91m) follow fingerpost ahead to **L** of house called Cobblers Row. Maintain direction along good field-edge path, with arable fields either side, to reach red-brick wall on **L**. Go along lawn of Well House and follow tarmac lane as it curves **L**.

❷ At corrugated barn of East Hall, follow Roach Valley waymark, **R** and then **L**, and maintain direction along good, grassy field edge. Walk by paddock fencing, with Church Hall on **R** and pond on **L**, to St Peter's Church at Paglesham Churchend.

❸ Keeping church on **R**, continue along Churchend High Street to Punch Bowl Inn. Maintain direction for 50yds (46m), take concrete path to **R** soon after 2 houses and after few paces continue along Roach Valley Way and follow public footpath sign, **L**, which soon becomes grassy field-edge path running parallel with waterway on **L**.

❹ Take short clamber up grassy embankment and, leaving Roach Valley Way, turn **R** on to sea wall of Paglesham Creek. Keep to path as it meanders by Paglesham Creek, which widens as you approach River Roach. To **L** salt marshes stretch towards River Crouch where you have views of marinas of Burnham-on-Crouch and warehouses and timber yards of Wallasea Island. Much of landward side of embankment is given over to sheep grazing which makes this walk somewhat difficult for larger dogs as enclosures are often divided by wooden stiles and low voltage electric fencing.

❺ As path bears **R**, with river on **L**, maintain direction past oyster beds to reach boatyard. Go down steps from sea wall and pick your way through boats and machinery to gate. Pass beside gate and follow unmade track to pass cottages on **L**, followed by Cobblers Row and fingerpost on **R** that was direction for outward journey. Turn **L** and return to The Plough and Sail pub at Paglesham Eastend.

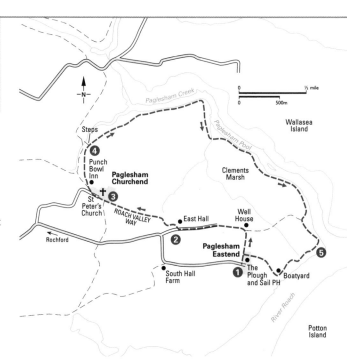

MALDON A Historic Route

Combine historic Maldon, home of salt making, with a network of waterways.

4.25 miles/6.8km 2hrs **Ascent** 115ft/35m ⚠ **Difficulty** ②

Paths Mainly grassy paths, narrow in parts and prone to mud after rain, some roads

Map OS Explorer 183 Chelmsford & The Rodings, Maldon & Witham **Grid ref** TL 853070

Parking Pay-and-display car park at Butt Lane

❶ From car park turn **L** and walk along Downs Road. Footpath drops quite steeply and soon you have views of River Chelmer and salt works. Where road curves **R** at riverside turn **L**, cross Fullbridge with care, and follow grassy embankment keeping river on **R**. Maintain direction and cross stile. Follow often muddy path, which meanders uphill through sloping meadow usually occupied by horses.

❷ Go through kissing gate and over adjacent stile and keep ahead, looking out for stile on **R** at top of hill. Turn **R** over stile. Turn immediately **R**, along downhill path through woodland and pass under A414 Maldon bypass. Continue along rising concrete path, and at end turn **R**.

❸ Maintain direction along this canopied green lane bounded by ancient hedgerows, and cross stile. Follow yellow waymark along grassy path keeping **L** to emerge on to gravel path.

❹ On **R** is Beeleigh Abbey. Continue past abbey and at end of road turn **R**. Ignore footpath on **L** and pass

Beeleigh Grange Farm on **L**, and Beeleigh Falls House, an impressive Victorian villa, on **R**. Go through kissing gate and soon you hear sound of rushing water of Beeleigh Falls.

❺ Cross timber bridge over weir. At end of bridge turn **R**, keeping river on **R**. Stop at 2nd weir for good river views. Continue, keeping river on **R**, and at Beeleigh Lock turn **R** and walk, with canal on **L**, towards red-brick bridge. Do not cross bridge, instead turn **R** on to concrete path and just before club house, **L** on to grassy path. Maintain direction with canal on **L** and the golf course on **R**. Cross next bridge and turn **R**, keeping canal on **R**. Continue under 2 sections of Maldon bypass and keep ahead on to grassy bridleway running parallel with canal.

❻ At next bridge take steps up to Heybridge Street. At top turn **R** and join B1018 towards Maldon. Maintain direction to cross River Chelmer via Fullbridge, bear **L** into Market Hill, turn **L** into High Street and return to car park via Butt Lane on **L**.

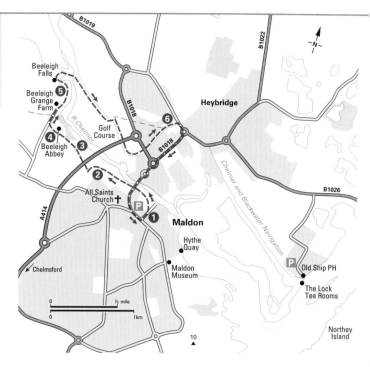

ROCHFORD Place Of The Peculiar People
Discover a tiny medieval town.

8 miles/12.9km 3hrs **Ascent** Negligible ⚠ **Difficulty** ⒉
Paths Grassy sea wall, field-edge paths and town streets
Map OS Explorer 176 Blackwater Estuary, Maldon **Grid ref** TQ 875904
Parking Pay-and-display at Back Lane

❶ Walk north between houses into Market Square and turn **R** into South Street, passing police station on **L**. By The Horse and Groom pub, turn **L** into Watts Lane following Roach Valley Way through industrial installations, with River Roach on **L** for 1 mile (1.6km).
❷ Follow path over bridge, with Stambridge Mill straight ahead. Follow concrete path around mill to reach Mill Lane. Turn **L**, and after 50yds (46m), turn **R** on to cross-field path to footbridge over fishing lake. Go through kissing gate and on to gravel path. Maintain direction through trees and across meadow, where on **R** you can see Broomhills house, former home of John Harriot, founder of Thames River Police.
❸ Follow waymark through kissing gate and join riverbank path. With river mudflats and salt marsh on **R**, continue ahead along grassy sea wall. Look **L** to see Saxon tower of church at Great Stambridge. Continue around peninsula of Bartonhall Creek, popular feasting ground of mudflats for migrating birds. Reaching northwestern tip, walk **L** down embankment to

fingerpost, leaving Roach Valley Way, and turn **L** towards Great Stambridge to pass old Essex barns converted into modern housing. Maintain direction along field-edge path towards houses and after 0.5 mile (800m) path passes Ash Tree Court and emerges on Stambridge Road. Turn **R** into Great Stambridge past The Royal Oak pub and notice attractive Victorian villas and post office.
❹ Just before post office, turn **L** into Stewards Elm Farm Lane and follow waymark over footbridge. Maintain direction between paddocks to kissing gate and turn **L** to follow field-edge path keeping Ragstone Lodge and Rectory on **L**. Continue on cross-field path following waymarks **R**, **L**, then half **R** past houses on **R**, to meet Stambridge Road.
❺ Turn **R** at The Cherry Tree public house and after about 200yds (183m), turn **L** into Mill Lane, then **R**, before houses, on to cross-field path to join Rocheway past houses and past The New Ship Inn on **R**. Turn **L** into South Street and return to car park.

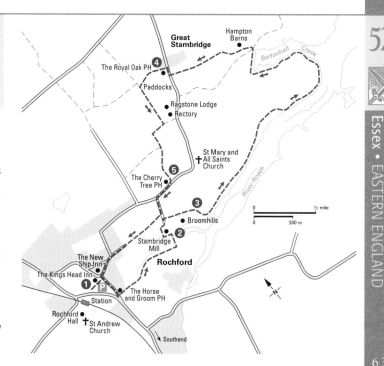

52

Essex • EASTERN ENGLAND

63

HANNINGFIELD RESERVOIR A Reservoir Trail
Walk through meadows and woodlands.

3.5 miles/5.7km 1hr 30min **Ascent** Negligible ⚠ **Difficulty** 1

Paths Grassy and gravel forest tracks, prone to mud after rains, some boardwalk

Map OS Explorer 175 Southend-on-Sea & Basildon **Grid ref** TQ 725971

Parking Free parking at the Visitor Centre, Hawkswood Road entrance. Gates close at 5pm

1 Go through Visitor Centre, take path ahead to waymark 1 and detour **L** for views of reservoir from Lyster Hide. Return to 1 and continue along path through Chestnut Wood for 100yds (91m). At waymark 3, bear **R** to clearing with picnic tables and then go ahead towards tall oaks and waymark 4. Keep ahead to cross wooden footbridge, passing pond on **L**, and continue to waymark 7 on edge of wood. Ahead are grazing meadows. Turn **L** along gravel path, keeping meadow on **R**, later following boardwalk on **R** to outdoor classroom in clearing with ponds and seating made from split trunks.

2 At waymark 8 turn **L**, passing waymark 9 to reach to Rawl Hide, for good views of reservoir and reed-covered embankment **L**. Now return to waymark 9, turn **L** on to wide grassy path to enter Peninsular Wood and continue to waymark 12. Bear **L** for 100yds (91m) and pass by Oak Hide to maintain direction to tip of peninsula and waymark 13, where you'll find Point Hide. Retrace steps

to waymark 12 and turn **L** in direction of Fishing Lodge with reservoir on **L**. Maintain direction passing waymarks 14 and 15 to cross concrete bridge.

3 Ignore stile across to Hawkswood and bear **L** to waymark 17 and enter Well Wood. Turn **L** and continue until you meet waymark 19, with Fishing Lodge and Water's Edge off **L**. Swing **R** and walk ahead, between coppiced trees with high embankment on **L** denoting old boundary of woods, to waymark 18. Turn **L**, keeping meadows on **R**, to waymark 24. Turn **L** to waymark 23 and **R** to waymark 22. Turn **R** again, into less dense woodland with South Hanningfield Road on **L**.

4 At waymark 25, continue to clearing of coppiced hornbeams, where path descends and goes past small ponds to waymark 26 passing waymark 27. Keep ahead to cross grassy track and just after waymark 28 bear **L** to enter Hawkswood. Keep ahead past waymarks 29 and 30 and at waymark 32, turn **R** cross wooden footbridge and go through kissing gates to return to car park.

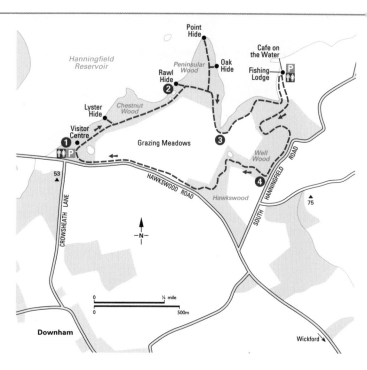

DANBURY Places And Palaces

Ancient woodland, meadows and lakes.

4 miles/6.4km 2hrs **Ascent** 164ft/50m ⚠ **Difficulty** 2

Paths Grass and woodland paths, field paths, some road

Map OS Explorer 183 Chelmsford & The Rodings, Maldon & Witham **Grid ref** TL 781050

Parking Free car park off Main Road opposite library and inside Danbury Country Park

① Leave car park via grassy path to **R** of leisure centre. Bear **R** along uphill path beside hedgerow and at crossing of paths by radio mast turn **L** and head downhill. Ahead are views of south Essex towards Kent.

② Turn **R** to pass The Cricketers Arms, then cross Bicknacre Road into Sporhams Lane. Follow path marked 'Butts Green'. At signpost on **R**, take track through dwarf oaks and gorse, to cross plank footbridge. After 25yds (23m), turn **R** along track, past houses.

③ At house called Dane View, keep **L** and follow footpath through woodland to Woodhill Road, and turn **L** to sign marking entrance to Danbury Country Park on **R**. In car park take kissing gate on **L** and go **L** again on to path just before information board.

④ Maintain direction past another car park and go through kissing gate on **L** before bridge. Pass to **L** of 2 lakes and, at toilets, turn **R** between lakes and continue ahead to red-brick perimeter wall of Danbury Conference Centre and Palace.

⑤ Turn **R** through formal gardens and, at end of 2nd lake, turn **L** though trees. Maintain direction uphill, diagonally across meadow and through kissing gate. From kissing gate, walk half **L** uphill towards copse. Continue to crossing of paths taking **R** path which soon passes to **L** of pond before reaching meadow. Cross meadow towards oak trees, following red and white posts.

⑥ At last white post, turn **L** and go through kissing gate carefully on to busy A414. Cross road into Riffhams Lane. At Elm Green Lane turn **R**, uphill, to A414 by war memorial on green. Turn **L**, cross road and turn **R** beside Rectory Farmhouse.

⑦ At T-junction turn **L** for views of St John the Baptist Church and graveyards. At 2nd T-junction, turn **L** to visit church. Turn **R** to rejoin outward path and return to car park.

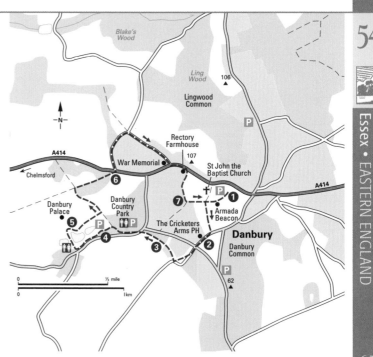

CASTLE HEDINGHAM Six Farms And A Castle

Explore a wealth of history in this tiny area.

3.5 miles/5.7km 1hr 30min **Ascent** 64ft/20m ⚠ **Difficulty** 1

Paths Grassy, field-edge and farm tracks, some woodland and town streets

Map OS Explorer 195 Braintree & Saffron Walden **Grid ref** TL 784356

Parking Informal street parking in Castle Hedingham village

❶ With church on **R**, walk along Church Ponds into Falcon Square with its medieval houses. Turn **L** into Castle Lane with 17th-century former Youth Hostel building on **R** and walk uphill to Bayley Street. Cross road and, at castle entrance, turn **R** and walk to T-junction. Turn **L** into Sudbury Road and, just after New Park Road on **R**, turn **L** at uphill narrow track to Rosemary Farm.

❷ Turn **L**, follow track to Y-junction and bear **L** passing red-brick, thatched Keepers Cottage on **L**. Pass houses and admire fine view of rolling countryside beyond stile on **L**, opposite Yeoman's cottage. After 200yds (183m) track bears **R** with converted barns of Rushleygreen Farm on **L**. Ignore timber footbridge immediately after farm and continue along main farm track with arable fields away to **L**.

❸ Pass Lippingwell's Farm on **R** and follow meandering field-edge path passing front of Newhouse Farm, with its pond on your **L**, and

continue to Hewson's Farm and brick-built tower on **R**. Turn sharp **L** at public footpath sign along field-edge path to small row of trees at rear of Newhouse Farm. At waymark bear **R** across fields to Kirby Hall Farm.

❹ Turn **L** at crossroads to Kirby Hall Road and, ignoring all footpaths **L** and **R**, follow this wide farm track passing hedgerows and rows of trees to return to Castle Hedingham. On way, pass through high embankments of hedgerows and impressive row of oak trees. Before rising towards village of Hedingham you can see top of castle keep, peering above trees to your half **L**.

❺ Walking into village, pass de Vere's Primary School and modern housing estate on **L**. At T-junction, turn **L** into Nunnery Street and **R** into Crown Street, where jettied buildings and medieval cottages herald your return to old village and church.

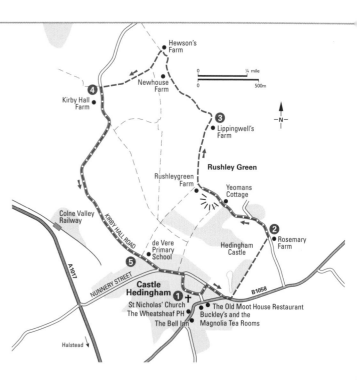

LANGDON An Old Plot For Eastenders

Explore ancient woodland and grassy meadows where Eastenders fulfilled a dream.

3.75 miles/6km 1hr 30min **Ascent** 230ft/70m ⚠ **Difficulty** 2
Paths Forest, field and horse tracks
Map OS Explorer 175 Southend-on-Sea & Basildon **Grid ref** TQ 659873
Parking Free parking at Langdon Visitor Centre, Lower Dunton Road

1 Walk up straight wide avenue of Plotlands signposted 'Plotlands Walk', passing museum on **L**. At crossing of paths by red waymark No 1, keep ahead through woodland path, with fields on **R**, and occasional views of south Essex between trees. Ignoring other paths, continue along this bridlepath and at metal fence look **L** for recreation ground. Continue along path for 100yds (91m) to wide cross paths.

2 Turn **R** at red waymark No 2. Now in Lincecewood, path undulates through high trees and open woodland, passing behind houses on **L**, and red waymark No 3.

3 Ignore steps by red and white marker on **L** and at waymark No 4 beside four steep wooden steps, then turn **R** along path, keeping wooden fencing enclosing Hall Wood on **L**. Walk for 20yds (18m), to break in trees and go over stile for views of London skyline. Retrace your steps and take 1st path on **L** downhill, towards wooden barrier, beside Nature Reserve sign.

4 Follow this narrow track down through ferns, after 200yds (183m) reach duckboard skirting pond. Note oak growing forming low arch across duckboard. Continue ahead through kissing gate and walk downhill as path meanders and undulates through open woodland, with ferns and patches of meadow awash with bluebells in spring. Continue along this path to wooden bench beneath large oak tree, where there are superb views of rolling farmland and London in distance.

5 50yds (46m) ahead, at Y-junction, take **L-H** path downhill keeping arable field on **L**. Go through pair of timber posts and turn **L** on to wide grassy bridleway. After footbridge beside barrier turn **R** and after 20yds (18m) turn **L** on to another grassy path. Pass beside wooden gate and maintain direction through 2 meadows, keeping houses on **R**. At end of 2nd meadow pass beside barrier, turn Rand ahead is red waymark No 1. Here, turn **R** keeping Plotland ruins on **L**. Pass Plotland Trail waymarks 5 and 6, turn **L** at next bridle path and follow waymarks back to car park.

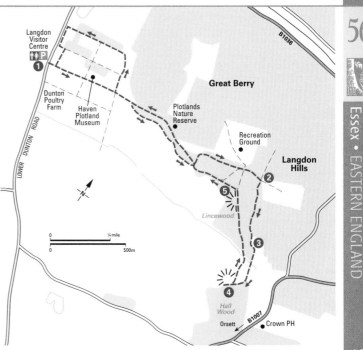

WEALD COUNTRY PARK A Royal Deer Park

A fairly strenuous walk taking in a great Tudor mansion and a royal deer park

5 miles/8km 2hrs 15min **Ascent** 117ft/35m ⚠ **Difficulty** ②
Paths Open parkland, forest tracks and some cross-field footpaths
Map OS Explorer 175 Southend-on-Sea & Basildon **Grid ref** TQ 568941
Parking Free car parks at Visitor Centre, Belvedere and Cricket Green on Weald Road and Lincolns Lane

❶ With your back to Weald Road, turn **R** out of car park past fingerpost beside parks office hut. Keep red-brick wall on **R** and continue to Belvedere car park – site of foundations of Weald Hall. Walk into car park and take earth path uphill between trees. Bear **L**, keeping church on **R**, and pass door which used to give access to graves of Tower family. At end of church wall, turn **L** through trees and go on to grassy knoll. This overlooks original gardens of estate and site of Weald Hall.

❷ Keeping gardens to **L**, walk up steps to site of Belvedere Hill where there is information house. Spectators would watch hunting and indulge in banquets. Walk down steps, turn **R** and take path downhill, between conifers, to open parkland. Maintain direction and go through gate on **R** and continue, keeping Bluebell Pond and cricket field on **R**.

❸ Follow grassy path uphill, passing bridleway waymarks on **R**. At top of hill, pass through thickly wooded area of ancient hornbeam and silver birch,

and continue along bridleway, which runs parallel with Sandpit Lane.

❹ As path veers away from road, note steep embankment **R** – remains of Iron Age settlement. You are walking around what was the moat. Keep to path through meadow and parkland and, at tree-clad embankment rising **R**, continue clockwise to join track.

❺ Turn **L** through tree gap to walk downhill beside fence. Pass to **L** of house. Cross footbridge and keep ahead through wood. Go through kissing gate on **R** and turn **R** along wide, grassy path. At path junction turn **R** by red and white post and turn **L** at yellow waymarked post. Turn **L** just after barrier and follow bridleway that borders Shepherd's Spinney.

❻ At next crossing of paths by barrier keep ahead, passing **L** of grassland. After 800yds (732m) turn **R** before kissing gate to walk with lake on **L**. At end of lake, turn **L** over footbridge and return to car park passing deer paddock.

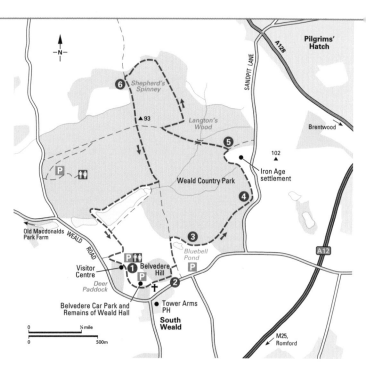

WILLINGALE A Pint-Sized Parish

An easy stroll along the Essex Way to a lovely rural village.

3.75 miles/6km 1hr 30min **Ascent** 33ft/11m ⚠ **Difficulty** ☐1
Paths Field-edge paths, riverside meadows and green lane
Map OS Explorer 183 Chelmsford & The Rodings, Maldon & Witham **Grid ref** TL 597076
Parking Free car park at Willingale Village Hall

❶ With your back to village hall, turn **R** following road around to **L** and turn **R** at footpath sign by former village school, now private residence. At end of gardens, keep ahead to **R** of hedge and follow grassy path as it curves **R**, to reach Dukes Lane. To **L** are panoramic views of Roding Valley.

❷ Turn **L** into Dukes Lane and after passing house called McKerros look out for where you turn **R** at public footpath sign. Walk up embankment and maintain direction along field-edge path with stream on **R** for about 400yds (366m). At hedge gap on **R** turn **L** along uphill cross-field path, go over plank footbridge by hedge gap. Cross another field, further footbridge and maintain direction until to junction with Elms Farm Road on **L**, and Elm Cottage over to **R**.

❸ Turn **R** on to bridleway, pass Elm Cottage and continue for 1 mile (1.6km), ignoring pair of footbridges. At T-junction turn **R** along track and at next T-junction turn **L** and then **R** at waymarked post

to join Essex Way. Follow this wide byway south, passing Windmill Farm on **L** to reach Shellow Road.

❹ Cross road and continue along Essex Way, with views of Shellow Hall to **L**. After 300yds (274m), cross plank footbridge, turn **R** and later **L**, keeping hedgerow to **R**. After another 100yds (91m), turn **R** through gap in hedge, then continue with hedgerow on **L**.

❺ In front of cottages at Spains Wood, cross footbridge over ditch and turn **R**, continuing along Essex Way. After earth bridge, maintain direction keeping hedgerow on **L**. Follow path through cricket field and into Willingale where Essex Way continues past The Bell on **R** (now private house) and crosses churchyard between St Christopher's and St Andrew's churches. After exploring churches and churchyard retrace your steps to The Street, which becomes Beech Road and return to village hall car park.

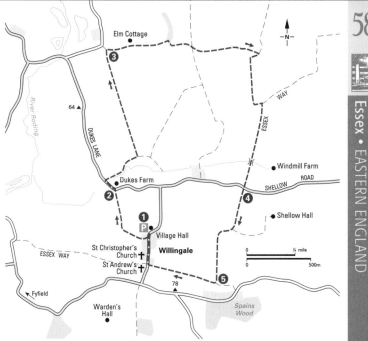

PLESHEY A Crowning Castle

A gentle walk combining rolling countryside and a fine motte and bailey castle.

3 miles/4.8km 1hr 30min **Ascent** 56ft/17m ⚠ **Difficulty** 1

Paths Grassy tracks, field and woodland paths prone to muddiness, some roads

Map OS Explorer 183 Chelmsford & The Rodings, Maldon & Witham **Grid ref** TL 662142

Parking Free car park at the village hall

❶ From car park at village hall, walk to The Street and turn **R** passing Holy Trinity Church on **R** and The White Horse pub on **L**. After church you will see 16th-century gatehouse, behind which is convent, collectively they are known as the House of Retreat. Just after restored water pump turn **R** into Pump Lane. After 100yds (91m), on **L** you will see bridge over moat – entrance into earthworks of motte-and-bailey castle.

❷ With your back to castle, and keeping church to **R**, walk across cricket field to waymark beside wooden gate. Turn **R** along concrete path keeping field on **L**. Maintain direction, ignoring 2 footpaths on **R** and 1 on **L** by reservoir.

❸ At 3-way public footpath sign turn **L** and follow bridleway bounded by trees. This path, which may be very muddy after rain, passes by Fitzjohn's Wood affording good views of rolling countryside. Beyond the outline of Holy Trinity Church you can appreciate the advantage of the hillside location of Pleshey Castle.

❹ When level with old house on **R**, which was Fitzjohn's Farm, walk few paces to line of trees by waymark on **L** and turn **L** on to field-edge path, downhill. Just after wooden footbridge over brook to **L** path curves **R** and then **L** beside wire fence. Keep ahead to cross plank footbridge over Walthambury Brook and continue up embankment so that brook is now **L**. You are now on grassy path of Essex Way, which follows Walthambury Brook to The Street at Pleshey.

❺ Turn **L** at The Street and turn **R** into Back Lane, passing Pleshey Hall Cottages on **L**. At signpost marked Pleshey Grange, turn **R** into Vicarage Road, passing site of former Pleshey Forge on **L**. At next public footpath sign, just after house called Pleachfield, turn **L** on to grassy path which follows Town Enclosure, with ditch on **L**. Cross footbridge and maintain direction to reach The White Horse pub on **L** and emerge into The Street. Turn **R** to return to car park.

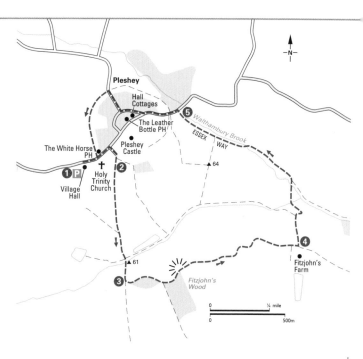

CHIPPING ONGAR David Livingstone
Home of missionary David Livingstone.

6.5 miles/10.4km 3hrs 30min **Ascent** 151ft/46m ⚠ **Difficulty** 2 **Paths** Track and field paths prone to muddiness, stretches of road, 5 stiles **Map** OS Explorer 183 Chelmsford & The Rodings, Maldon & Witham and OS Explorer 175 Southend-on-Sea and Basildon **Grid ref** TL 552032 **Parking** Pay-and-display car parks at rear of Sainsbury's, police station and library in Chipping Ongar High Street

1 From rear of car park beside police station take Essex Way towards Greensted. As path narrows, walk between dwarf oaks, over cross path and through kissing gate and keep ahead, passing pond of Greensted Hall on your **R**. Walk through gate, passing Church Lodge on your **L**; Greensted church is on **R**.
2 Keeping church on **R**, bear **R** towards barn conversion and go through waymarked gate. After 100yds (91m), turn **L** across footbridge and follow field-edge path keeping hedgerow on **R**. Maintain direction through 3 fields, passing Greensted Wood on **R**, until you reach Greensted Road. Turn **L** and pick up footpath on **R**. Continue along field-edge path keeping hedgerows on **L** for about 100yds (91m); go through kissing-gate so that hedgerow is now on **R**. Negotiate stiles and squeezer stiles.
3 At 5th stile turn **R**, pass to **R** of Widows Farm and continue along enclosed path of The Essex Way. At Y-junction of paths take **L** path diagonally across

field to hedge. Keep hedge on **L** and continue ahead towards houses. Turn **R** along lane and at T-junction turn **L** towards Coleman's Farm.
4 As lane bears **R** into Coleman's Farm, maintain direction on to bridleway for 0.5 mile (800m), ignoring paths **L** and **R** to reach tarmac lane. Just before T-junction, turn **R** on to cross-field path to Stanford Rivers. At converted barn dwellings on **L**, turn **R** on to gravel path then **L** on to School Road with St Margaret's Church on **L**.
5 Walk past church to crossroads and turn **L**. After 400yds (366m) follow **R** turn next to house (Ambermead). Maintain direction on uphill path for views of farmland and pass ridge of oak trees at Kettlebury Spring. Follow path past school and turn **R** to reach The Borough. Continue to T-junction passing the Two Brewers pub on **R**. Turn **L** into High Street and return to car park.

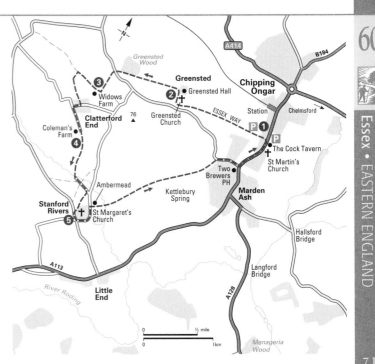

GREAT BARDFIELD A Windmill Called Gibraltar

Gentle hills, a windmill and a lovely village.

4.5 miles/7.2km 2hrs **Ascent** 100ft/30m ⚠ **Difficulty** ☐ 1

Paths Field-edge paths, river bank, grassy tracks and some town streets, 4 stiles **Map** OS Explorer 195 Braintree & Saffron Walden **Grid ref** TL 677305 **Parking** Informal parking in Great Bardfield village

❶ From war memorial opposite The Vine pub walk down hill passing the Quaker Meeting House to village green. Turn **L** at public footpath sign, follow path by public footpath sign and then follow path by stream on **L** with houses on **R**. After 200yds (183m) at field, take **L** fork still following stream. Look over your **R** shoulder for good view of Gibraltar Windmill.

❷ Cross stile through hedge, turn **R** and continue with hedge on **R** to reach lane at Great Bardfield Watermill. Cross lane and keep mill pond and River Pant on **L** and pass to **L** of pumping station. Go over stile and take cross-field path keeping river and Champions Farm and Robjohns Farm on **L**. Cross earth bridge and stay on grassy path through arable farmland keeping river on **L-H** side and crossing footbridge by waymark post and stile. Go through gate and cross stile to lane.

❸ Turn **R** uphill passing Whinbush Farm. At junction of Bardfield–Waltham road, bear **R** following green public footpath sign. Cross 2 stiles; maintain direction

along path that skirts edge of Lodge Wood. Cross another stile and after 100yds (91m) look for where you turn **R** at waymark. Keeping wood on **L**, continue to next waymark and turn **R** beside hedgerow.

❹ Follow path by hedge under row of poplar and larch trees and, as outline of Great Bardfield and windmill come into view, turn **L**. Follow track with hedgerows on **L** for about 300yds (274m) and turn **R** into green lane.

❺ Walk past recreation ground on **R**, cross residential street and follow footpath into Braintree Road; turn **R**. On **L** is Church of St Mary the Virgin with its Norman tower and 14th-century nave.

❻ Next to church is 16th-century manor house of Bardfield Hall, and for more of Great Bardfield's history follow road **L** through Brook Street, passing starting point of walk into High Street. In quick succession you can see Gobions, one of the oldest houses in the village, Place House, the Cottage Museum and the Town Hall. Retrace your steps to green.

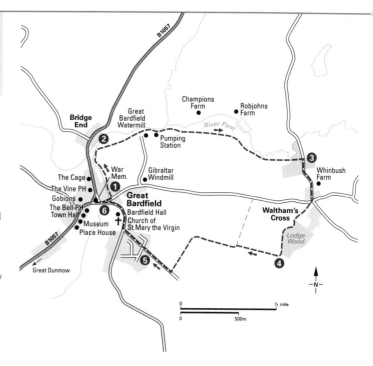

THAXTED The Sound Of Music

In the footsteps of composer Gustav Holst.

3 miles/4.8km 1hr 30min **Ascent** 92ft/28m ⚠ **Difficulty** 1

Paths Field-edge paths, bridleway prone to muddiness, river bank and some town streets

Map OS Explorer 195 Braintree & Saffron Walden **Grid ref** TL 610311

Parking Free car park at Margaret Street

❶ From car park turn **L** into Margaret Street, **R** into Weaverhead Lane and **L** into Copthall Lane, passing row of cottages called Bridgefoot. After houses on **L**, pass through gap between trees by gate marked 'Walnut Tree Meadow'. Turn **R** along grassy path and keep parallel with Copthall Lane on **R**. After 400yds (366m) bear **L** at yellow waymark through trees, cross 2 footbridges at right angles, in quick succession, and turn **R** keeping stream and hedgerows on **R**.

❷ Maintain direction along field-edge path through 2 fields. After spinney on **L**, turn **L** at waymark over footbridge and follow another field-edge path keeping hedgerow on **L** and crossing another footbridge to B1051, Sampford Road. In distance, to **L** is spire of St John the Baptist Church. Turn **R**, cross road with care, and take 1st **L** turning along farm track 'Boyton End'. Track zig-zags **L** and **R** past Sorrell's Farm House and Goldens Farm. At Golden Farm bear **R** on to narrow canopied bridleway between buildings, and later bear

R along field edge. Turn **L** outside Goddards Farm and follow track downhill.

❸ Cross road to farm and adjacent track to follow fingerpost through hedge. Turn half **L** across field and follow path with River Chelmer on **R** to Walden Road.

❹ At Walden Road turn **R** across Armitage Bridge and immediately **L** at public footpath sign (now following Turpin's Trail). Follow field-edge path with river on **L** passing conifers and, after 300yds (274m), turn **L** at waymark concealed in hedgerows. You are now on Harcamlow Way. Continue downhill along driveway leading from house called Haslemere, and go over concrete bridge across river. Ignore paths **L** and **R** and continue along tarmac road, past elegant modern housing surrounded by rolling countryside.

❺ Continue along Watling Lane passing 17th-century cottages and Piggot's Mill until you emerge opposite The Swan. Turn **L** and **R** into Margaret Street and return to car park.

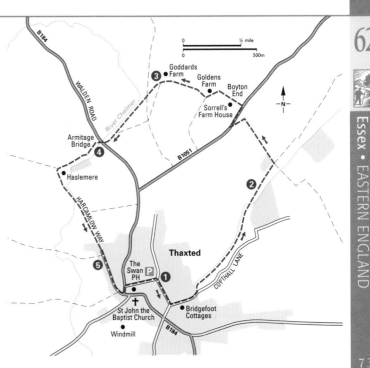

SAFFRON WALDEN To Audley End
A challenging walk to Audley End.

5.5 miles/8.8km 2hrs 30min **Ascent** 180ft/55m ⚠ **Difficulty** 2
Paths Urban, field-edge, grassy tracks
Map OS Explorer 195 Braintree & Saffron Walden **Grid ref** TL 534384
Parking Long stay at Swan Meadow

❶ From Swan Meadow car park follow 'town centre' sign into Park Lane turning **R** to go through small archway of almshouses. Turn **R** into Abbey Lane and go through wrought iron gates of Audley End Park. Maintain direction along grassy path to top of hill, and exit via another set of wrought iron gates, to Audley End Road.

❷ Turn **R** along embankment and go downhill for 600yds (549m), keeping red brick wall of Audley End Park on **R**, to reach fingerpost marked 'College of St Mark'. Cross road and turn **L** to Audley End village.

❸ Cross bridge and turn **L** at lane marked 'Abbey Farm private' and continue along this footpath keeping St Mark's College, followed by farm, to **R**. Maintain direction along concrete drive, cross Wenden Road and go through trees to join Beechy Ride (track). Keep stream and line of beech trees **R** for 200yds (183m). Cross earth bridge between trees, and continue with stream and trees now to **L** to B1052. Cross road with

care, and continue along footpath opposite, along edge of field with stream on **L**. At earth bridge turn **L** and immediately **R** so that stream is now on **R**.

❹ Follow field-edge path until it abuts Brakey Ley Wood and ignore 3 sets of waymarks indicating **R** turns. At 4th waymark, continue along field-edge path to Debden Road.

❺ Turn **R** at Debden Road and, opposite The Roos, turn **L** on to byway and then immediately **L** along uphill path. Bear **L** at Herberts Farm and **L** again to rejoin Debden Road. Turn **R** towards Claypits Plantation and maintain direction into Seven Devil Lane.

❻ After 0.5 mile (800m) turn **R** on B1052 towards Saffron Walden. At roundabout bear **L** across road and follow footpath between houses later passing deep ditch on **L**, which is part of ancient defence system. At end of path turn **R** into Abbey Lane and car park.

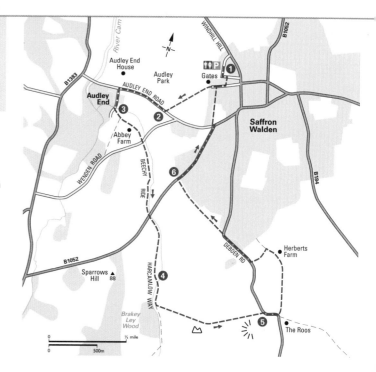

HARLOW Old And New

A stroll exploring town and country from Mark Hall to Old Harlow.

4 miles/6.4km 1hr 30min **Ascent** 67ft/20m ⚠ **Difficulty** ☐1

Paths Cycle tracks, footpaths, sections of road, 1 stile

Map OS Explorer 174 Epping Forest & Lee Valley **Grid ref** TL 465109 **Parking** Free car park at Harlow Museum off Fesants Croft, open Tuesday to Sunday. Otherwise plenty of on-street parking

❶ Turn **L** outside Harlow Museum, continue along Muskham Road; follow cycle path sign to Templefields and Old Harlow. Turn **R** and follow cycle path under A414 and into Old Harlow. Continue along Market Street to T-junction and turn **L** at The Chequers pub into Station Road. After 300yds (274m), turn **R** into Swallows estate, take 1st **L** and follow footpath through recreational park to Manor Road. Turn **L** then **R** into Priory Avenue passing corporation houses, the first to be built in the early days of Harlow new town, until you come to crossroads with Old Road.

❷ Turn **R**. To **L** you can see 12th-century Harlowbury Chapel. This Norman chapel is thought to be the oldest intact building in Harlow. Maintain direction to reach T-junction opposite Green Man pub and hotel. Here turn **R** and take footpath between old ambulance and fire station and walk field-edge path. Just before main road, turn **L** between concrete posts and follow footpath to B183. Bear half **L**, cross road and follow footpath through trees and bear **L** on to field-edge path. After

200yds (183m), cross stile and footbridge and walk towards spire of St Mary's and St Hugh's Church to reach graveyard; continue ahead through churchyard.

❸ Turn **R** into Churchgate Street passing 17th-century Widow's House – inscribed with dedication by landowner's wife to pair of poor widows – followed by The Queen's Head pub and other timber-framed houses. Continue downhill to footpath on **R** just before Swallow Churchgate Hotel. Cross bridge and keeping church and stream on **R**, follow field-edge path to pass barrier. Bear half **L** across meadow through break in fence opposite beside redundant stile and, keeping trees and stream on **R**, continue to kissing gate at top of hill.

❹ Pass outbuildings of Old Harlow Kennels and Cattery on **L** and follow tarmac road to London Road. Turn **R** into London Road and cross just before roundabout on to B183 to next roundabout on A414. Follow underpass into First Avenue/Mandela Avenue. Cross road and take narrow path on **R** by signpost to Harlow Museum.

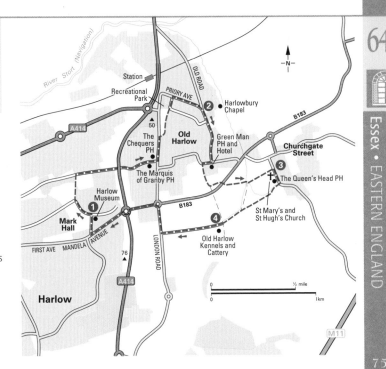

64

Essex • EASTERN ENGLAND

75

GILWELL PARK Scouting Around

The woodland GQ of the Scout Association.

6 miles/9.7km 2hrs 30min **Ascent** 231ft/70m ⚠ **Difficulty** 3
Paths Grassy paths, forest tracks, green lanes, some stretches of road, several stiles **Map** OS Explorer 174 Epping Forest & Lee Valley **Grid ref** TQ 387963 **Parking** Free car park in Gilwell Lane

① From Wilson Way visitor car park pass to **L** of The White House and turn **R** to pass through gates of Gilwell Park following yellow waymark. Keep to wide grassy path between trees and the Scout Association buildings. At top of hill there are panoramic views of the reservoir. Follow steep downhill path with wood and pond on **R** and go through squeezer stile to emerge beside village hall at Sewardstone.

② Turn **L** into Dawes Hill and **L** again into Sewardstone Road. Turn **R** into Mill Lane passing houses and maintain direction on downhill track towards King George's Reservoir. Turn **R** and follow track, with reservoir and Horsemill Stream on **L**, to footbridge over stream.

③ Do not cross bridge. Go straight through gate and turn **R** on to waymarked London Loop path, walking east to reach Sewardstone Road. Turn **R** and after 100yds (91m), turn **L** over stile and ignore London Loop path **R**. Walk up steep north flank of Barn Hill, stopping to look around occasionally at tremendous views over reservoirs, Epping Forest and Waltham Abbey.

④ After crossing gravel path and stile opposite this, turn **R** on to wide Green Lane. Maintain direction and turn **L** at 2nd public footpath signpost marked 'Lippitts Hill'. Follow yellow waymark posts across golf course, later bearing **L** past police firearms training camp fence on **R**; don't be alarmed if it sounds as though there's a war going on. The marksmen are well away from you.

⑤ At Lippitts Hill, turn **R** passing training camp and The Owl pub, the gardens of which afford lovely views across Epping Forest. 50yds (46m) after pub turn **R** at public footpath signpost, go up wooden steps and on to steep downhill path via steps. Maintain direction between horse paddocks and cross wooden footbridge and another stile. Follow path over undulating meadow across flank of hill, then downhill to houses on **L**. At public footpath sign to Sewardstonebury go through metal gate and follow line of oak trees across West Essex Golf Course. Maintain direction across fairways and past houses to emerge via stile into Bury Road. Turn **R**, then 1st **L** to return to car park.

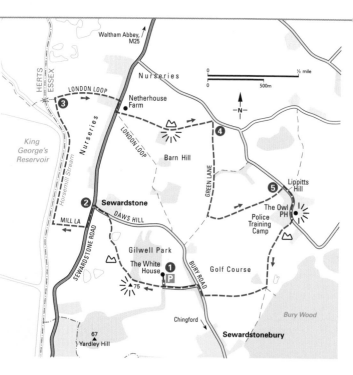

WALTHAM ABBEY Lee Valley Park

Gunpowder mills, woodland and waterways.

7.5 miles/12.1km 4hrs **Ascent** 269ft/82m ⚠ **Difficulty** 3

Paths Grassy riverside, steep field paths, green lanes prone to mud after rain, short stretch of road, 5 stiles **Map** OS Explorer 174 Epping Forest & Lee Valley **Grid ref** TL 384015

Parking Free car park at Cornmill Meadows, closes at 6pm

❶ From rear of car park, take gravel path to information board and go straight ahead through woodland. At Cornmill Stream turn **R** with stream down on **L-H** side and views across Cornmill Meadow. At footbridge turn **R** following perimeter fence of Waltham Abbey Royal Gunpowder Mills.

❷ Keep fence on **L** to 'Hooks Marsh' fingerpost. Path then curves **L** across field towards alder woodland. Turn **R** along field-edge path with brook on **L**, to stile. Turn **L** on to Fishers Green Lane, which leads to car park and information board.

❸ Cross 2 footbridges over streams and go through kissing gate on **R** signposted 'Fishers Green'. Follow gravel path bounded by Seventy Acres Lake on **L**.

❹ After 600yds (549m) at signposts indicating 'Lea Valley Park farms and Fishers Green', cross metal footbridge and turn **L** through picnic area. Follow riverside path to emerge at tarmac road to car park. Walk through this and turn **L** along tarmac road to Fishers Green Sailing Club.

❺ Pass Crannum Hide and just before sailing club entrance turn **R**, cross stile beside gate and walk along field-edge path keeping sailing club on **L**. Keep to path as it bears **R** uphill to another stile.

❻ At top of hill look back for wonderful views of north London and Hertfordshire. Follow footpath sign for Clayton Hill, cross wooden bridge and turn **R** to Coleman's Shaw. Turn **R** on to B194 and follow road as it goes downhill.

❼ At T-junction, turn **L** at Coach & Horses pub into Waltham Road. Cross carefully and walk uphill past Denver Lodge Farm on **R**. Cross stile on **R** and follow field-edge path to Galleyhill Wood. Cross next 2 stiles and continue, keeping woods on **R**, to break in trees. Walk through and at cross path turn **R** on to green lane to Galley Hill Green. Here, turn **R** and after 100yds (91m), turn **L** in front of houses to join Claygate Lane to emerge beside Eagle Lodge. Cross Crooked Mile Road to meadow and turn **L** through kissing gate and return to car park.

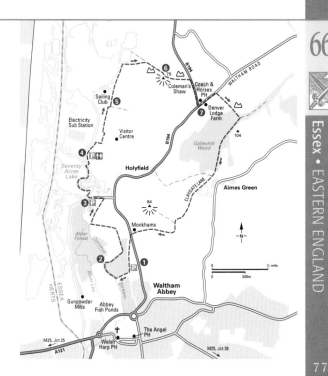

SOMERLEYTON Great Victorian Entrepreneur
Around the delightful estate village designed by a flamboyant Victorian railway magnate.

6.25 miles/10.1km 2hrs 30min **Ascent** 131ft/40m **⚠ Difficulty** 2
Paths Farm tracks, field-edge paths, country lanes, 2 stiles
Map OS Explorer OL40 The Broads **Grid ref** TM 484972
Parking On-street parking outside Somerleyton post office

❶ With back to post office, turn **L** past estate cottages towards green. Turn **L** to walk around green; continue around outside of school. Return to road, turn **L** along pavement opposite red-brick wall of Somerleyton Park.
❷ Follow road round to **L** and turn **R** on lane signed 'Ashby'. After 300yds (274m), turn **R** past thatched lodge at pedestrian entrance to Somerleyton Hall. Pass through gates and keep on this lane for 400yds (366m), then turn **L** on to field-edge path.
❸ After 300yds (274m), turn **R** on to farm track. Stay on waymarked path as it swings **L** through farmyard and continues alongside 2 fields, then turns sharp **R** towards wood. Turn **L** to walk along edge of wood and keep to path as it bends around pond and enters small belt of woodland. Keep **R** through woods and cross stile, then look for 2nd hedge gap to **R** and bear half **L** on cross-field path to hedge and lane on other side.
❹ Turn **R** and stay on this lane for 1 mile (1.6km). Just before road junction, take field-edge path to **L** and

follow this round to gap in the wall. Cross B1074 and climb stile to keep ahead on field-edge path for almost 0.75 mile (1.2km).
❺ Turn **R** at end of track along Waddling Lane. Path drops down towards water-meadows with railway and River Waveney to **L**. When path divides, fork **L** to climb around edge of Waddling Wood. Keep ahead when track joins from **L** to head uphill and away from woods.
❻ Turn **L** opposite Waveney Grange Farm and walk towards station. Turn **R** opposite station entrance on wide track. When track bends **R**, keep **L** on grassy path down to boatyard. Turn **L** around buildings to marina, then turn **R** past marina and climb access drive to road.
❼ Turn **L** and walk along pavement as far as Duke's Head pub. Stay on this road as it bends to **R**. At next bend, by black railings of cottage, turn **R** on waymarked path. Follow this path along edge of field and turn **R** beyond telegraph pole, past houses. At kissing gate, turn **L** to return to start of walk.

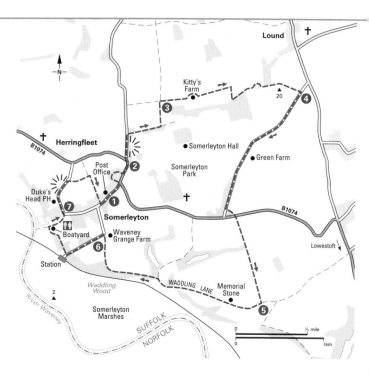

COVEHITHE The Crumbling Cliffs

See the effects of coastal erosion on a walk along a rapidly disappearing cliff top.

4.5 miles/7.2km 1hr 45min **Ascent** 131ft/40m ⚠ **Difficulty** ☐1☐
Paths Cliff top, shingle beach, farm track and country lanes, 1 stile
Grid ref TM 522818 **Map** OS Explorer 231 Southwold & Bungay
Parking On street near Covehithe church

❶ Take tarmac lane from church down towards sea. Reach barrier with 'Danger' notice and sign warning that there is no public right of way. Although this is strictly true, this is a well-established and popular path stretching north towards Kessingland beach and you are likely to meet many other walkers. The warnings are serious but it is quite safe to walk here so long as you keep away from the cliff edge.

❷ Walk through gap to **R** of road barrier and continue towards cliffs, then turn **L** along wide farm track with pig farm to **L**. Path follows cliff top then drops down towards beach to enter Benacre nature reserve. On **L** is Benacre Broad, once an estuary, now a marshy lagoon. Like others on the Suffolk coast, the shingle beach here attracts little terns in spring and summer and you should keep to the path to avoid disturbing their nesting sites.

❸ Climb back on to well-worn path on cliffs at end of Benacre Broad. Way cuts through pine trees and bracken on constantly changing path before running alongside field and swinging **R** to drop back down to

beach level where you should take wide grass track on **L** across dunes.

❹ When you reach concrete track, with tower of Kessingland church visible in distance, turn **L** following waymarks of Suffolk Coast and Heaths Path. Go through kissing gate and keep straight ahead, passing Beach Farm on **R**. Stay straight ahead for 1 mile (1.6km) on wide track between fields with views of Benacre church up ahead.

❺ Go through steel gates and turn **L** on to quiet country lane. Stay on this lane for 0.75 mile (1.2km) as it passes between hedges with arable farmland to either side and swings **L** at entrance to Hall Farm.

❻ When road bends **R**, turn **L** past gate. Stay on this path as it swings **R** around meadow and continues into woodland of Holly Grove. Pass through another gate and turn **L** along road for last 0.75 mile (1.2km) back into Covehithe. Turn **L** at junction to return to church.

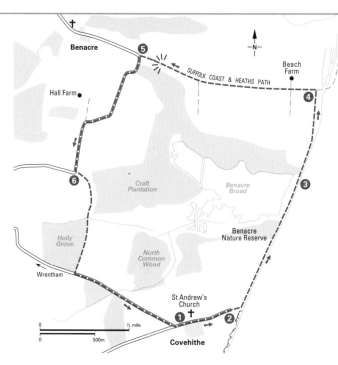

SOUTHWOLD From The Pier

A walk around this old-fashioned holiday resort on an island surrounded by river, creek and sea.

4 miles/6.4km 1hr 30min **Ascent** Negligible ⚠ **Difficulty** ☐1
Paths Riverside paths, seaside promenade, town streets, 2 stiles
Map OS Explorer 231 Southwold & Bungay **Grid ref** TM 511766
Parking Beach car park (pay-and-display) or free in nearby streets

1 Leave pier and turn **L** along seafront, either following promenade past beach huts and climbing steps or walking along clifftop path with views over beach. After passing St James' Green, where pair of cannon stand either side of mast, continue along clifftop path to Gun Hill, where 6 more cannon, captured at the Battle of Culloden near Inverness in 1746, can be seen facing out to sea.

2 From Gun Hill, head inland alongside large South Green, then turn **L** along Queen's Road to junction with Gardner Road. Cross this road, then look for Ferry Path footpath, that follows pleasant stream beside marshes towards river. Alternatively, stay on clifftop path, and walk across dunes to mouth of River Blyth.

3 Turn **R** and walk beside river, passing Walberswick ferry, group of fishing huts where fresh fish is sold, and Harbour Inn. After about 0.75 mile (1.2km), you reach iron bridge on site of old Southwold-to-Halesworth railway line.

4 Keep straight ahead at bridge, crossing stile and following path round to **R** alongside Buss Creek to make complete circuit of island. There are good views across the common to Southwold, dominated by the lighthouse and the tower of St Edmund's Church. Horses and cattle can often be seen grazing on the marshes. Keep straight ahead, going over stile, through gate to cross embankment, then over another stile. Stay on raised path to reach white-painted bridge.

5 Climb up to road and cross bridge, then continue on path beside Buss Creek with views of beach huts in distance. Path skirts boating lake on its way down to sea. Turn **R** and walk across car park to return to pier.

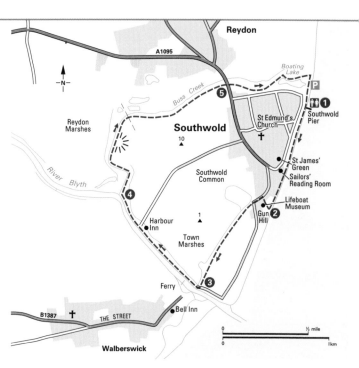

ALDEBURGH Benjamin Britten

On the trail of Benjamin Britten.

5.75 miles/9.2km 2hrs 30min **Ascent** Negligible ⚠ **Difficulty** ☐
Paths River and sea wall, meadows, old railway track
Map OS Explorer 212 Woodbridge & Saxmundham **Grid ref** TM 463555
Parking Slaughden Quay free car park

❶ Start at Slaughden Quay, once a thriving port, now a yacht club. Walk back briefly in direction of Aldeburgh and turn **L** along river wall on north bank of River Alde. There are good views to your left of the Martello tower that marks the northern end of Orford Ness. Stay on river wall for 2 miles (3.2km) as river swings to **R** towards Aldeburgh.

❷ When river bends **L**, go down wooden staircase to **R** and keep straight ahead across meadow with water tower visible ahead. Go through gate and bear half **L** across next meadow to cross footbridge. Next, follow waymarks, bearing half **R**, then keep straight ahead across next field to reach another footbridge. After crossing 5th footbridge, path runs alongside allotments and goes through gate to reach lane.

❸ Turn **L** by brick wall and cross recreation ground. Continue past fire station to reach road. Turn **R** for 75yds (69m) then go **L** on signposted footpath almost opposite hospital entrance. Follow this path between houses, cross road and keep straight ahead with caravan site on **R**.

❹ When you see footpath on **R**, leading to track across caravan park, turn **L** and immediately **R** on permissive path that follows trackbed of old railway. Stay on this path for 0.5 mile (800m) as it climbs steadily between farmland to **L** and woodland and marshes to **R**. Turn **R** at junction of paths to open meadows. Stay on this path, crossing North Warren nature reserve with views of Sizewell power station to **L**.

❺ Cross road and turn **R** along tarmac path that runs parallel to beach. As you approach Aldeburgh, pass striking scallop sculpture on shingle (erected in 2003 to celebrate Benjamin Britten's life in Aldeburgh), fishermen's huts and fishing boats that have been pulled up on to the shingle. Pass timber-framed Moot Hall and continue along Crag Path, past lifeboat station and pair of 19th-century look-out towers. At end of Crag Path, bear **R** across car park and walk around old mill to return to Slaughden Quay.

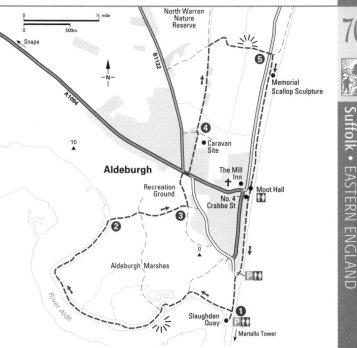

SOUTH ELMHAM Through Saints Country

Wide views and huge expanses of farmland on a walk through scattered parishes.

8.75 miles/14.1km **4hrs** **Ascent** 295ft/90m ▲ **Difficulty** 3

Paths Field paths, meadows and country lanes, 3 stiles

Map OS Explorer 231 Southwold & Bungay **Grid ref** TM 306833

Parking South Elmham Hall free car park (when closed, start from St Peter's Hall)

❶ From car park, walk between trees and cross moat on permissive path. Take footbridge over stream and keep ahead across meadow. Go through gate and turn **L** along green lane enclosed by hedges. At junction of tracks, turn **L** to cross footbridge and through kissing gate. Walk across meadows to admire the minster.

❷ Continue ahead along line of hedge and turn **L** at end of next meadow to cross footbridge and climb on field-edge path. Turn **R** at road and after 300yds (274m) turn **L** on to quiet lane. Follow this lane as it bends to **R** and continue for 0.75 mile (1.2km).

❸ Cross main road and keep straight ahead on grassy field-edge path. Pass through hedge, cross next field and turn **R** beyond hedge. Walk beside this hedge for 0.5 mile (800m) to junction; turn **R** on to cross-field path that becomes wide track. Turn **L** at crossroads and walk across fields with water tower to **R** to reach St Michael's Church.

❹ Turn **L** along road. After 0.5 mile (800m), cross humpback bridge and stay on this road to St Peter's Church. Follow road round to **R** past entrance to St Peter's Hall, then turn **L** across plank bridge to walk beside moat. Path swings **R** then **L**, following line of hedge between open fields.

❺ At junction of paths, turn **L** along field-edge track, waymarked 'Angles Way'. This soon becomes grassy lane and then pebbled farm drive. Cross road and keep straight ahead on concrete track.

❻ Turn **L** at next road to pass Mushroom Farm and, in 300yds (274m), go **R** on field-edge path. After 0.5 mile (800m), reach junction of paths with half-white, half-weatherboarded farmhouse visible to **R**. Turn **L** to climb towards small wood and continue through woods. Go through gate, cross stream, go through another gate and climb green lane to road.

❼ Turn **L**, then **R** in 300yds (274m) on to lane signposted 'South Elmham Hall'. Follow this lane round to **R** to return to start.

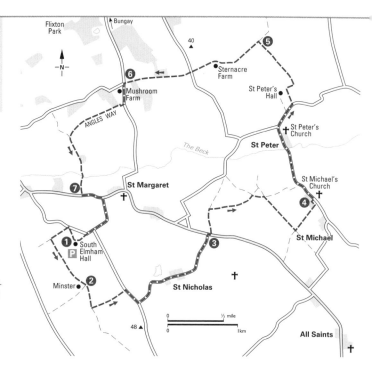

DEBENHAM Historic County Town

Exploring the green lanes and pathways around a historic county town.

6 miles/9.7km 2hrs 30min **Ascent** 197ft/60m ⚠ **Difficulty** 2
Paths Field-edge and cross-field paths, country lanes
Map OS Explorer 211 Bury St Edmunds & Stowmarket **Grid ref** TM 174631
Parking Cross Green free car park, High Street, Debenham

❶ Walk away from High Street past butcher and fork **R** at Priory Lane to cross River Deben. Turn **R** at road and, after 100yds (91m), turn **L** on sloping cross-field path. Pass through hedge and continue around field edge before turning **L** along country lane.

❷ At junction of bridleways, ignore 'Circular Walk' signs and keep straight ahead on oak-lined drive to Crows Hall, which takes its name from Debenham family crest. Follow waymarks around to **R** of farm, pass bungalow and turn **L** beside hedge on to field-edge path. Go **L** again at end of field and stay on this path as it crosses footbridge to **R** around Great Wood. After another 250yds (229m), turn **L** across fields to come to wide track signposted 'Bridle Way'. Turn **R** here; turn **R** along lane to pass large farm buildings of Grove Farm, then Crowborough Farm.

❸ At start of line of telegraph poles, turn **L** alongside hedge on to grassy path. Stay on this path for 0.5 mile (800m), passing wind pump and pair of water towers

before descending to cottage with wooden barns.

❹ Turn **L** along Waddlegoose Lane. Stay on this green lane for about 1.75 miles (2.8km). Where obvious track bends **R** at house, stay straight ahead on field-edge path next to hedge. At junction bear **R**. Path is now enclosed by tall hedges, obscuring your view of fields.

❺ At next junction, turn **R** along farm track and stay on this track past converted barn and brick farmhouse. Turn **L** along road for about 400yds (366m), then turn **R** on to bridle path signposted 'Circular Walk'. After passing through gate, path goes around Hoggs Kiss Wood, one of 200 community woodlands created for millennium. You can either stay on path or walk down through woods and meadows.

❻ Reach end of Hoggs Kiss Wood, turn **R** around allotments and fork **R** along Water Lane to High Street. Turn **L** along High Street to return to start of walk.

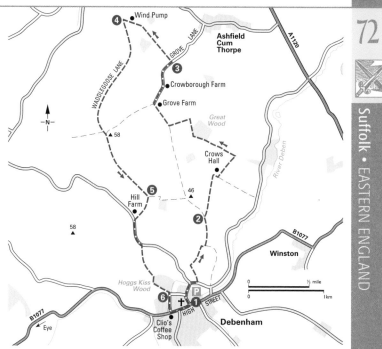

WOODBRIDGE Down By The River

Along the River Deben from a riverside town.

4 miles/6.4km 1hr 30min **Ascent** 164ft/50m ⚠ **Difficulty** 1

Paths River wall, riverside paths, town streets, some steps

Map OS Explorer 197 Ipswich, Felixstowe & Harwich or 212 Woodbridge & Saxmundham

Grid ref TM 271485 **Parking** The Avenue car park, Woodbridge

❶ Leave car park on The Avenue and cross railway line to continue to boatyard at end of lane. Turn **R** to walk along river wall, passing slipways of Deben Yacht Club. Continue along river wall on easy section of walk, on tarmac path with lovely views out over meadows **R** to enter National Trust-owned land at Kyson Hill.

❷ Turn **L** at 3-way junction to drop down to beach; walk along foreshore beneath oak trees. (If tide is high, you may have to turn **R** instead, picking up route at Point 4.) Keep **R** at wooden railings and follow this path round to Martlesham Creek, where you scramble up embankment and follow peaceful riverside path.

❸ Turn **R** at end of creek and around sewage works to Sandy Lane. Turn **R** beneath arched railway bridge and stay on this road as it climbs steadily for about 700yds (640m). At top of rise, turn **R** on to Broom Heath.

❹ When road bends round to R, turn **L** past gate leading to Woodland Trust woods (Porter's Wood). (The short cut rejoins from **R** here.) Stay on path on outside

of woods to return to Sandy Lane. Turn **R** here and **R** again at main road, then cross road and climb steps on far side after 50yds (46m). Keep ahead to end of this footpath and cross road to reach Portland Crescent.

❺ Keep ahead to drop down hill and climb up other side. Continue along Fen Walk, enclosed by black railings with graveyards to either side. Fork **L** at junction of paths to drop down grassy slope with views of church tower up ahead. Keep straight ahead and climb steps to Seckford Street.

❻ Turn **R** and stay on this road to reach Market Hill. Alleyway on **R-H** side leads you to churchyard. Turn **L** through churchyard on to Church Street, emerging alongside site of old abbey, now private school. Walk down Church Street and cross over The Thoroughfare, attractive pedestrian shopping street, on **L-H** side. Continue walking along Quay Street and cross station yard to take footbridge over railway line. Once over, turn **L** to visit Tide Mill or **R** to return to start of walk.

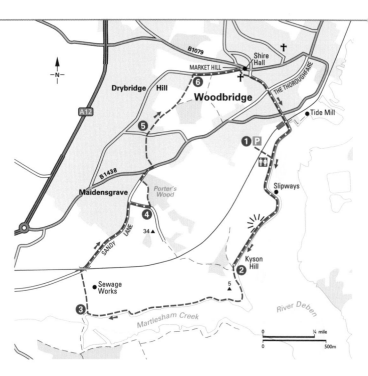

SUTTON HOO A Warrior's Grave

By the site of a pagan burial ground.

7.25 miles/11.7km 3hrs **Ascent** 262ft/80m ⚠ **Difficulty** ②

Paths Field-edge and riverside paths, farm lanes, short section of busy road
Map OS Explorer 197 Ipswich, Felixstowe & Harwich **Grid ref** TM 290493 **Parking** National Trust car park
– included in entry price for exhibition, or pay-and-display when exhibition closed (free to NT members)

❶ From car park, take signposted blue trail from behind visitor centre, descending towards River Deben on gravel track. Turn **L** opposite entrance to Little Haugh and turn **R** by map of Sutton Hoo Estate. Path narrows and turns **L** alongside fence on its way to river. Keep **L** around meadow and climb steps to riverbank with Woodbridge visible on opposite bank.
❷ Turn **L** and walk along riverbank. Path is overgrown in places and plank bridges can be slippery in wet weather but views are superb. After 400yds (366m), climb steps to **L** to leave river behind and turn **L** around turf field. Keep to field edge as it swings **R** and climbs between woodland to **L** and reservoir to **R**.
❸ Turn **R** at top of rise to follow bridleway along field edge with Deben Wood to **L**. At end of wood, path swings half **L** across field, then passes through hedge on to lane. You could turn **L** here for short cut, picking up walk again in 300yds (274m) at Point ❻.
❹ Keep straight ahead for 0.75 mile (1.2km), crossing

drive to Haddon Hall. At Methersgate Hall bear **R** around farm buildings, then **L** on footpath beside brick wall. Pass pair of cannon on lawn of hall and continue ahead with River Deben opening out ahead. Go through gate and turn **L** across field then go through another gate and turn **R** along lane. Stay on this lane for 1 mile (1.6km) and as it bends **L** past Cliff Farm.
❺ At 2nd 3-finger signpost turn **L** along field-edge track, passing embankment on R. Keep to public bridleway as it swings **L** around area of woodland. At end of woodland, keep straight ahead between fields and continue as path becomes broad grass track through trees, passing cottages to reach minor lane.
❻ Turn **R** and stay on this lane for about 1 mile (1.6km) to main road (B1083). Turn **L** and walk carefully along verge for 400yds (366m), soon to take footpath **L** opposite road junction. When you see burial mounds to **L-H** side, turn **R** to return to visitor centre on National Trust permissive path.

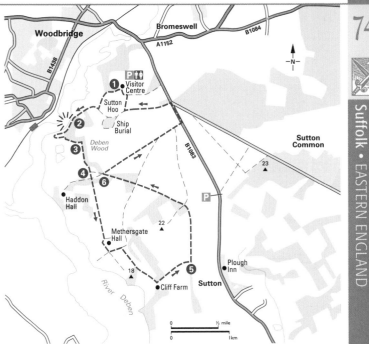

EAST BERGHOLT Constable Country

A gentle walk through the landscape that inspired one of England's greatest artists.

3.75 miles/6km 1hr 30min **Ascent** 246ft/75m ⚠ **Difficulty** 1

Paths Roads, field paths and riverside meadows, 7 stiles

Map OS Explorer 196 Sudbury, Hadleigh & Dedham Vale   **Grid ref** TM 069346

Parking Free car park next to Red Lion, East Bergholt

❶ Turn **R** out of car park, pass Red Lion pub and post office, then turn **R** along lane, noting Constable's early studio on **L**. Continue along this lane, past chapel and cemetery, through gate and down **L** side of meadow to cross footbridge. Climb path on far side for marvellous views of Stour Valley and church towers at Dedham and Stratford St Mary.

❷ Turn **L** at junction of paths to walk down Dead Lane, sunken footpath. At foot of the hill, turn **L** on to field-edge path. Path goes **R** then **L** to cross stile on edge of Fishpond Wood. Walk beside wood for few paces, then climb another stile into field and walk beside hedge to **R**. Path switches to other side of hedge and back again before bending **L** around belt of woodland to Fen Lane.

❸ Turn **R** along lane, crossing cart bridge and ignoring footpaths to **L** and to **R** as you continue towards wooden-arched Fen Bridge. Cross bridge and turn **L** to walk beside River Stour towards Flatford on wide open pasture of flood plain.

❹ Cross bridge to return to north bank of river beside Bridge Cottage. Turn **R** here, passing restored dry dock on way to Flatford Mill.

❺ Walk past Willy Lott's House and turn **L** past car park. Optional loop here, on National Trust permissive path, leads **R** around outside of Gibbonsgate Field beside hedge. Otherwise, keep **L** on wide track and go through gate to join another NT path through Miller's Field. Stay on this path as it swings **L** and climbs to top of field, then go ahead through kissing gate. Keep ahead, ignore stile on **L** and soon follow fenced path to T-junction of footpaths. Turn **L** here along track to rear of barns and continue down drive of Clapper Farm to Flatford Road.

❻ Turn **R** along road. At crossroads, turn **L** passing the King's Head pub and Haywain Restaurant on way back to East Bergholt. Stay on pavement on **R** side of road to walk through churchyard and return to start of walk.

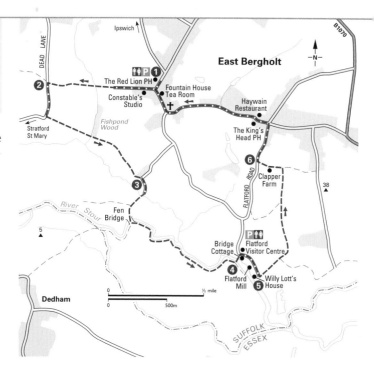

SHOTLEY Between Two Rivers

Views of Harwich and Felixstowe from a spit between the Stour and Orwell estuaries.

6 miles/9.7km 3hrs **Ascent** 262ft/80m ⚠ **Difficulty** 2

Paths Field and riverside paths, country lanes, 2 stiles
Map OS Explorer 197 Ipswich, Felixstowe & Harwich **Grid ref** TM 246336
Parking Opposite Bristol Arms at Shotley Gate

❶ Start at Bristol Arms, looking across to Harwich, and head **L** along waterfront to Shotley Marina. Pass to **R** of HMS Ganges Museum (open summer weekends) and keep **R** to walk across lock gates to Shotley Point. Path follows headland around marina basin, with good views of Felixstowe Docks. Turn **R** to continue along flood bank between marshes and mudflats. After 1 mile (1.6km) path passes old oyster beds and swings **L** beside salt marshes at Crane's Hill Creek.
❷ Half-way around creek, where you see 3-finger signpost, descend bank to **L** and cross stile to join meadow-edge path. Cross stile and bear **L** along track to climb past vineyards to St Mary's Church.
❸ Walk straight ahead at crossroads beyond church, on tarmac lane leading to Shotley Hall, then turn **L** on to cross-field path opposite drive. Follow this path diagonally across field, then bear **R** at far corner, following line of telegraph poles towards road where you turn **L**.

❹ After 50yds (46m), turn **R** along lane, signposted 'Erwarton Walk'. At end of this lane, turn R, passing red-brick Tudor gatehouse of Erwarton Hall. Stay on this quiet country road as it bends towards Erwarton village. Just after **R-H** bend, turn **L** beside churchyard on to wide track. Pass to **R** of cottage and turn **L** along field-edge path with fine views over River Stour.
❺ At end of field, turn **R** and follow field-edge down to River Stour. Turn **L** and follow Suffolk Coast and Heath Path beside river, eventually passing cottages and property called Stourside.
❻ Continue between fields and river and soon climb gently through trees to houses and road. Follow road and keep straight on along tarmac path where road curves **L**. Join another road and follow this to T-junction. Turn **R** downhill back to The Bristol Arms on **L**.

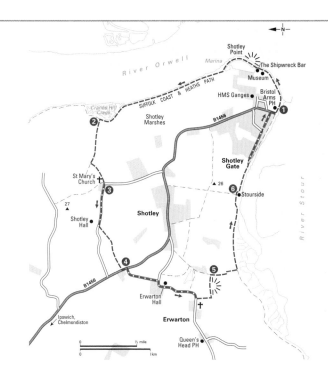

FELIXSTOWE FERRY Fish And Ships

A pleasant walk along the Deben Estuary reveals another side to Felixstowe.

6.5 miles/10.4km 3hrs **Ascent** 164ft/50m ⚠ **Difficulty** ②

Paths Field and riverside paths, country lanes, farm tracks, sea wall, 4 stiles

Map OS Explorer 197 Ipswich, Felixstowe & Harwich **Grid ref** TM 328376

Parking Ferry Café car park (fee), Felixstowe Ferry

❶ Take tarmac path along embankment behind Ferry Café car park. Path passes boatyard and follows river wall as you look down on abandoned boats lying moored in muddy flats. Turn **R** through squeeze stile to walk beside Deben Estuary. After 0.5 mile (800m) path swings **L** and then **R** across inlet at entrance to King's Fleet.

❷ Turn **L** to descend embankment and walk along broad track. You pass old wind pump and stay on this track as it winds its way between farmland and King's Fleet. After 1 mile (1.6km) track bends **R** and climbs to farm where it becomes tarmac lane. Continue to T-junction.

❸ Turn **L** across field to climb to ridge then drop down through next field to The Wilderness, belt of trees beside Falkenham Brook. Turn **L** through trees and follow this path alongside stream, then bend **R** to cross stile and meadow. Make for corner of hedge opposite and bear **R** alongside fence to cross

footbridge and continue on grassy path between fields. At end of field, turn **L** and continue to end of hedge, then turn **R** to climb track to Brick Kiln Cottages.

❹ At top of track, turn **L** along lane and stay on this lane past Gulpher Hall and its duck pond. As road bends **R**, walk past entrance to The Brook and turn **L** on field-edge path. Path ascends then turns **R** around field and cuts straight across field corner, unless it's diverted by crops. Pass through gate and keep straight on along lane, then turn **L** before houses in 150yds (137m) to join another path that runs between fields.

❺ At pill box, turn **R** on to Ferry Road. Cross Cliff Road and turn **L**, walking past clubhouse and turning half **R** across golf course on signposted path to reach sea wall. Turn **L** and walk along wall, passing 2 Martello towers and beach huts. Continue to mouth of estuary and turn **L** just before jetty to return to Ferry Café.

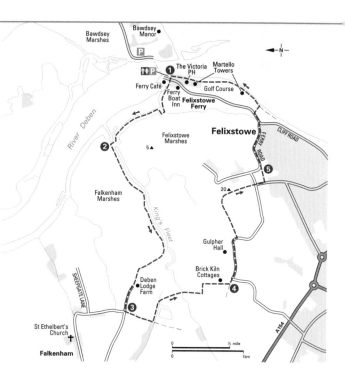

GIPPING VALLEY Wildlife Wander

A walk along a peaceful valley, looking out for herons, kingfishers and otters.

5 miles/8km 2hrs **Ascent** 213ft/65m ⚠ **Difficulty** 2

Paths Riverside, field-edge and cross-field paths, 12 stiles

Map OS Explorer 211 Bury St Edmunds & Stowmarket **Grid ref** TM 123512

Parking Gipping Valley Centre

❶ Follow signs from Gipping Valley Centre to river. Path crosses play area, climbs embankment, crosses road and descends on far side. Turn **L** alongside fence then bear **R** between fishing lakes. Turn **R** again to walk under railway bridge and continue along Gipping Valley River Path.

❷ Turn **L** to cross bridge at Great Blakenham Lock. Follow Gipping Valley River Path markers to turn **R** between houses and take narrow passage beside Mill Cottage to return to river. Stay on riverside path for 1.5 miles (2.4km). Pass beneath railway line and cross quarry access road to reach wider stretch of river with water-meadows to L. Pass lock and keep ahead at Causeway Lake. Continue around edge of meadow, ignoring footbridge to **R**. Shortly after, cross stile and bear R, following course of river. Walk around another meadow with views of rare breeds farm, then cross footbridge and follow narrow path to Baylham Mill.

❸ Turn **L** across bridge. Cross railway line and turn **R** at road. After 200yds (183m), cross road and walk through hedge to pass around back of Moat Farm. Keep ahead on wide track. Turn **L** then **R** to climb between fields to plateau with isolated oak and sweeping views. Turn **L** then **R** on to field-edge path with hedge to **R**.

❹ Turn **L** on field-edge path to drop Upper Street. Path swings **L** through kissing gate in hedge and **R** across meadow. Go through gate and walk down lane past church and old school.

❺ At foot of Church Lane, turn **L** and immediately **R** by sign 'No horses please'. Path crosses farmland and briefly enters Devil's Grove before emerging opposite Walnut Tree Farm. Turn **L** along lane and **R** by pond to pass through gate and cross meadow. Go through another gate and keep walking ahead on cross-field path, then follow 'circular walk' signs and keep **R** on farm track. Turn **L** to walk into Great Blakenham.

❻ Cross B1113 and walk along Mill Lane. Road bends **L** to return to Point ❷, where you can retrace your steps to car park at start of walk.

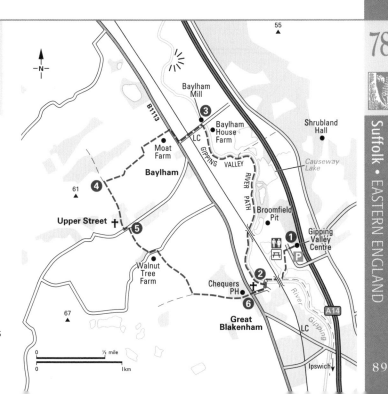

HOXNE A Thousand-Year Tree
Around the village where the last King of East Anglia met his untimely death.

3.5 miles/5.7km 1hr 30min **Ascent** 197ft/60m ⚠ **Difficulty** ☐1
Paths Country lanes, field and woodland paths, 2 stiles
Map OS Explorer 230 Diss & Harleston **Grid ref** TM 179769
Parking Hoxne village hall

❶ Turn **L** out of car park to cross Goldbrook Bridge, noting inscription: 'King Edmund taken prisoner here, ad 870'. Turn **R** to cross tributary of River Dove and pass Swan Inn on **L**. Fork **R** to climb past post office alongside village green and continue to top of lane to arrive opposite Church of St Peter and St Paul.

❷ Turn **R** along road and take 2nd **L**, Watermill Lane. Bear **R** along tarmac and chippings lane with 'No through road' sign. Lane drops into valley beside water-meadows of River Waveney which marks border between Norfolk and Suffolk. At mill entrance drive, turn **R** on to another concrete track that swings to **L** past huts to become green lane bordered by hedges. Turn **R** on field-edge path with house to **L**, then **R** on to tarmac lane. Turn **R** at end of lane to return to main road.

❸ Turn **L**, walk around bend and turn **R** on to Wittons Lane, also signposted 'Hoxne Cross Street'. After crossing stream, turn **R** through kissing gate to enter Brakey Wood, new woodland created to commemorate the millennium. Keep to **R** alongside stream and walk around edge of woods before going through kissing gate to reach sewage works.

❹ Keep ahead on footpath along field edge. St Edmund's Monument is in field **R** and it is usually possible to reach it on permissive footpath. Cross plank footbridge and stay on public footpath as it bends to **R** around 2nd field and enters belt of woodland. Arrive at Cross Street by small garage and shop.

❺ Maintain direction, walking ahead for another 60yds (55m). When road bends sharply **R**, continue ahead on public footpath between houses which then turns **L** around field. Path turns **R** and **L** to cross ditch and drops down steeply beside next field with tall hedge on **L-H** side. Cross stile, turn **R** and in about 50yds (46m), go **L** over footbridge. Pass through gate and keep walking ahead on sloping cross-field path to meet road.

❻ Turn **R** and walk along road to return to Goldbrook Bridge.

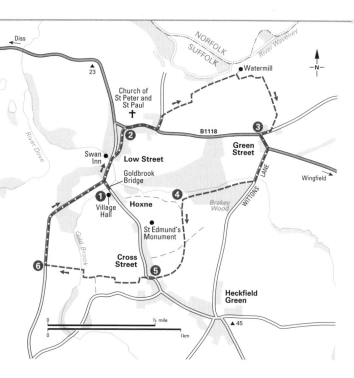

SUDBURY Oil On Canvas
On the trail of Thomas Gainsborough.

5 miles/8km 2hrs **Ascent** Negligible ⚠ **Difficulty** 1️⃣
Paths Old railway track, meadows and town streets
Map OS Explorer 196 Sudbury, Hadleigh & Dedham Vale **Grid ref** TL 875409
Parking Kingfisher Leisure Centre (free)

1 Leave car park through gate at start of Valley Walk, then turn **L** to walk around Friar's Meadow. Cross meadow and turn **R** to follow bank of Stour, then turn **R** alongside tributary and climb steps to rejoin Valley Walk.

2 Turn **L** and cross footbridge, noting Quay Theatre, housed in old maltings, to **R**. You now stay on Valley Walk for 2 miles (3.2km). At first path is enclosed between tall embankments but, after passing Stour Valley Path sign and crossing Belchamp Brook, it opens out to reveal views of arable farmland and meadows.

3 Just before reaching road junction, climb steps of embankment on **R**, cross paddock and turn **R** along driveway to Borley Hall. Look for narrow footpath between high garden wall of hall and Borley Mill, the 1st of 3 former watermills on route. Go through gate to cross small meadow to further gate, then turn **L** beside stream. Cross footbridge and walk across meadow to road at end of enclosed path.

4 Turn **R** along pavement for 250yds (229m). Just beyond Chaucer Road on **L**, turn **R** on to tarmac lane

with views of North Meadow Common to L. Cross bridge to pass Brundon Mill and turn **L** alongside pink cottages. Soon you are on Sudbury Common Lands among horses and cattle. Walk across meadow, passing World War II pill box, then cross footbridge and bear half **R** across Fullingpit Meadow. Metal bridge leads into Freemen's Common, where you bear half **R** towards old white-painted mill, now converted into Mill Hotel.

5 Pass through gate to walk beside hotel, then turn **R** and **L** along Stour Street, passing half-timbered buildings including 15th-century Salters Hall. Turn **R** along School Street past old grammar school, then **L** along Christopher Lane to emerge on Gainsborough Street opposite Gainsborough's House. Turn **R** to reach Market Hill, where statue of Thomas Gainsborough stands in front of St Peter's Church.

6 Turn **R** past Corn Exchange, now library, along Friars Street. After passing half-timbered Buzzards Hall, once owned by Gainsborough's uncle, look for passage on **L** that leads back to start of Valley Walk.

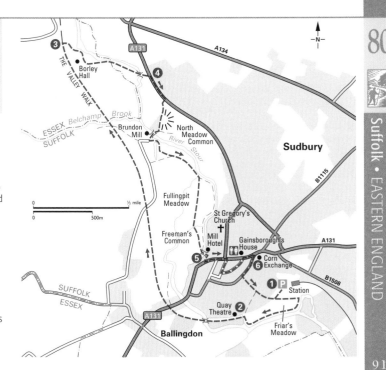

81

Suffolk • EASTERN ENGLAND

LONG MELFORD A Tudor Mansion

A walk through farmland and woods, by a Tudor mansion and a fine church.

6 miles/9.7km 2hrs 45min **Ascent** 213ft/65m ⚠ **Difficulty** 2
Paths Farm tracks, field and woodland paths, 7 stiles
Map OS Explorer 196 Sudbury, Hadleigh & Dedham Vale **Grid ref** TL 864465
Parking Church Walk, Long Melford

❶ Starting from Black Lion Hotel, walk up west side of green towards church, passing almshouses of Trinity Hospital. Bear **L** around church and walk through rectory garden. Cross stile, then turn **R** in few paces and cross paddock, heading for stile in corner. Cross another stile to reach meadow and continue straight ahead to reach long drive to Kentwell Hall.

❷ Turn **L** and walk beside avenue of lime trees towards Kentwell Hall. At main gate, turn **L** to walk through grounds with good views of hall. Follow waymarks to turn **R** beside hedge and continue ahead on wide track that crosses farmland with sweeping views to both sides. Ignore tracks leading off **R** and **L** and continue towards Kiln Farm.

❸ Just before derelict farm buildings, turn **R** on to track running between fields and woods. At 2nd wood, Ashen Grove, turn **L** on to shady woodland path that crosses 2 grassy tracks and swings **R** through trees to emerge on to field-edge path. Continue ahead on

cross-field path, that cuts through hedge and makes its way across fields towards Bridge Street. Cross lane and walk past recreation ground, then go over pair of stiles to reach A134 by Rose and Crown pub.

❹ Cross main road carefully and take **L** fork opposite. Almost immediately, turn **R** on to path alongside Chad Brook. Stay on this path for about 1.75 miles (2.8km) as it crosses footbridge to west side of brook, then clings to stream between farmland to **R** and woodland to **L**. Ignore 1st path off to **R**. At end of woods, path suddenly swings **R** to climb around field edge and return to A134.

❺ Cross road again and keep straight ahead along Hare Drift, now concrete track. Reach Long Melford between garden centre and pub, directly opposite entrance to Kentwell Hall. Cross road, turn **L** and walk back down towards green.

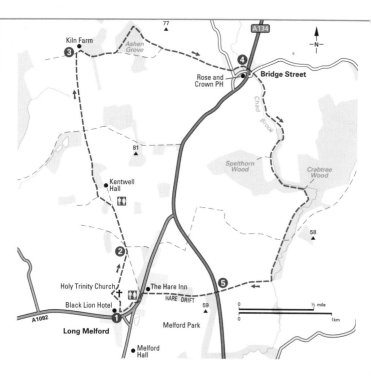

LAVENHAM Wool Town

A walk through picturesque medieval streets.

5.5 miles/8.8km 2hrs 30min **Ascent** 197ft/60m ⚠ **Difficulty** ②
Paths Field-edge paths and tracks, some stretches of road
Map OS Explorers 196 Sudbury, Hadleigh & Dedham Vale; 211 Bury St Edmunds & Stowmarket
Grid ref TL 914489 (on Explorer 196) **Parking** Church Street car park (free), Lavenham

❶ Turn **R** out of car park and go down hill into town. At 1st junction, turn **R** along Bear's Lane. Continue on road for 0.25 mile (400m) until last house, then take footpath to **R** across fields. After another field boundary in 0.25 mile (400m), turn **L** in next field and follow ditch to rejoin road.

❷ Turn **R** and walk past Weaner's Farm. Turn **L** at footpath sign just before converted barn. Stay on this path as it swings around Bear's Lane Farm; turn **L** on to track beside hedge. Walk along this track as it bears **R** to valley bottom. When track bends **R** towards Abbot's Hall, keep ahead and fork to **R** on grassy path beside stream.

❸ Emerging from poplar grove, arrive at concrete drive; turn **R** and immediately **L**. Path swings round to **R** to reach Cock Lane. Turn **L** and stay on this road as it climbs and then descends to crossroads.

❹ Cross A1141 into Brent Eleigh. When road bends, with village hall and half-timbered Corner Farm to **R**,

keep ahead to climb to St Mary's Church. Look into the church to see the late 13th-century wall paintings and 17th-century box pews. Continue up same road.

❺ When road swings sharply to **R**, look for path on **L**. Stay on this path for about 1.25 miles (2km) as it winds between tall hedges with glimpses of open countryside. Emerging into daylight, there is a wonderful view of the church tower at Lavenham standing proudly above the town. Walk past Clayhill Farm and descend into valley, crossing white-painted bridge.

❻ Turn **L** at junction and walk into Lavenham along Water Street, with its fine timber-framed houses. Just after Lavenham Priory on **L**, turn **R** up Lady Street, passing tourist office on way to market place. Turn **L** down Market Lane to arrive at High Street opposite picturesque Crooked House. Turn briefly **L** and then **R** along Hall Road. Before road bends, look for footpath on **L**, then walk through meadow to reach Lavenham church. Car park is across road.

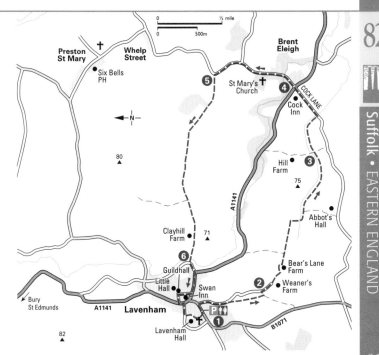

HARTEST Picture-Book Village

Discover a link with a well-known nursery rhyme on the rooftop of Suffolk.

5 miles/8km 2hrs **Ascent** 394ft/120m ⚠ **Difficulty** ☐2

Paths Quiet country roads, footpaths and bridleways

Map OS Explorer 211 Bury St Edmunds & Stowmarket **Grid ref** TL 833525

Parking Hartest village hall

❶ Turn **L** out of car park and cross road to reach village sign. Continue along south side of green, passing Crown Inn and All Saints Church. Keep on this road as it bends **R**, leaving village behind to climb Hartest Hill. Along way you pass peaceful burial ground.

❷ At public footpath leading off **R**, pause at summit of Hartest Hill to admire extensive views over High Suffolk and Hartest nestling in its own little valley. Stay on this road for 0.75 mile (1.2km). Turn **R** at junction to reach Gifford's Hall and continue ahead until the next bend in road.

❸ When road swings **L** at Dales Farm, keep ahead on bridleway, which clings to hedges and field edges as it descends towards Boxted. When you reach road, turn **R** to walk into village itself.

❹ Turn **L** when you see sign to Boxted church. Cross bridge over River Glem and stay on this road as it climbs out of village. About 0.5 mile (800m) after leaving Boxted, you reach church, hidden among trees,

with views over Boxted Hall from churchyard. Retrace your steps into Boxted (for short cut, you could leave this section out, but you would be missing one of high points of walk). Returning to start of Point ❹, turn **L**, pass electricity substation and keep **L** towards Hawkedon when road divides.

❺ Approaching 1st house on **L**, look for public footpath, half-hidden between tall hedges to **R**. This path is known as Roger's Lane. At times it can become very muddy and overgrown, in which case simpler alternative is to go back to junction and return to Hartest by road. Otherwise, keep on this path as it ascends hill.

❻ When you get to top of Roger's Lane, turn **R** along road to descend into Hartest village, with more wonderful views. Road ends at village hall, which was erected by Thomas Weller-Poley in 1888.

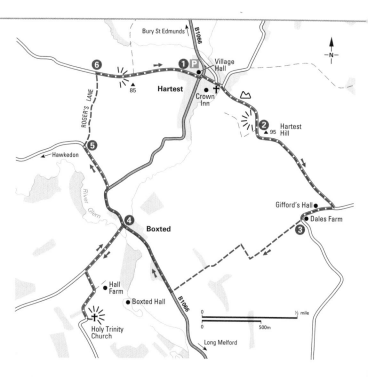

MOULTON A Border Walk

An enjoyable walk in rolling downland.

6.5 miles/10.4km 3hrs **Ascent** 295ft/90m ⚠ **Difficulty** 3
Paths Field-edge, cross-field and woodland paths, 9 stiles
Map OS Explorer 210 Newmarket & Haverhill **Grid ref** TL 696644
Parking Moulton village hall

❶ Turn **R** out of car park along Bridge Street, passing King's Head pub on your way to packhorse bridge. Cross bridge and turn **R** along Brookside, walking beside River Kennett. Just before Old Flint Bridge, notice old rectory school on **L**, dating from 1849. Keep on this road to churchyard.

❷ Go through gate to enter churchyard and pass St Peter's Church. Cross stile behind church and walk up through trees to another stile at top. Bear **R** across fields. On clear days, Ely Cathedral is visible on horizon to **L**.

❸ Reaching road, turn R. Keep ahead when road bends, walking between hedges of Gazeley Stud, where mares and foals can be seen. Continue on this path to All Saints Church and walk around rear of church to emerge by Gazeley village sign and Chequers pub.

❹ Walk down Higham Road, opposite church, and bear **R** following Icknield Way waymarks at Tithe Close. Walk between houses and follow this path

across fields and into Bluebutton Wood. Where path turns sharply **R**, look for footbridge in hedge to **L**.

❺ Keep on Icknield Way as it winds through 2 more woods, emerging beside wide field. Walk along field edge, up through trees to crossroads. Turn **R** here and climb to St Mary's Church, with Dalham Hall visible behind.

❻ Pass through metal kissing gate opposite church and walk down through avenue of chestnut trees to Dalham village. Go through kissing gate and turn **L**, noting large conical red-brick malt kiln standing beside road.

❼ Cross white footbridge to **R** and follow this path beside River Kennett. Reaching road, turn **R** across Catford Bridge. Now turn **L** on wide bridleway to return to Moulton at St Peter's Church.

❽ Cross Old Flint Bridge and walk across green to Dalham Road. Turn **R** along this road. Gate opposite post office leads to recreation ground and back to village hall.

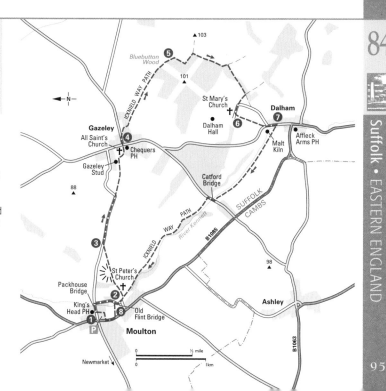

HORSEY MERE Silent Windmills

Explore whispering reed beds and windmills and finish at a National Trust pub.

3.5 miles/5.7km 1hr 30min **Ascent** Negligible ⚠ **Difficulty** 1
Paths Marked trails along dykes (walk quietly to avoid disturbing nesting birds), 5 stiles
Map OS Explorer OL40 The Broads **Grid ref** TG 456223
Parking National Trust pay-and-display at Horsey Drainage Mill

❶ From car park walk towards toilets and take footpath to **R** of them to footbridge. Cross, turn immediately **R** and follow path alongside Horsey Mere through reeds and alder copses. Cross wooden bridge across dyke and through gate to enter grassy water-meadow. Look for white disc across field. Go through 2nd gate and over bridge.

❷ Turn **R** when path meets brown-watered dyke (Waxham New Cut). Eventually, you will see derelict Brograve Drainage Mill ahead. Herons and other birds often perch on its sails, so it's worth stopping to look.

❸ Turn **R** immediately adjacent to mill and walk along field edge. Reed beds give way to water-meadow. Cross plank bridge and continue ahead. Path bends **L**, then **R**, then crosses small lane and continues through field opposite. At end of field, make sharp **L**, eventually reaching lane.

❹ Go R, bearing **R** where lane meets track, and walk past Poppylands Café. At junction turn **L**, following sign for Nelson Head. Pass pub on your **L-H** side, then look for well-defined footpath going off **R**.

❺ Walk past gate and continue along wide sward ahead, with narrow dyke on either side. When sward divides, bear **L** and head for stile at end of footpath. Climb this and immediately turn **R** to walk along spacious field. This area is used for grazing breeding stock and you should look for signs warning about the presence of bulls. This part of walk is permissive, and not public footpath; the NT is within its rights to put bulls here. Check for warning signs. These are always prominently displayed. If this is the case, you will have to walk back to lane and turn **L**. This will return you to car park at start.

❻ Assuming there are no bulls to hinder your progress, climb stile, between field and road, and then cross road. Car park where walk began is ahead and slightly to **R**. This is a good time to explore restored Horsey Drainage Mill, just to **L**.

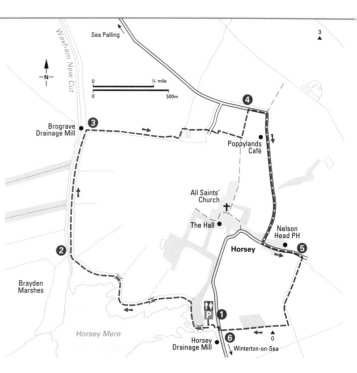

LUDHAM The Broads

Enjoy the windmill-studded skyline in this lovely stroll to the River Ant.

5 miles/8km 2hrs **Ascent** 33ft/10m ⚠ **Difficulty** 2
Paths Quiet country lanes and grassy footpaths
Map OS Explorer OL40 The Broads **Grid ref** TG 391180
Parking Womack Staithe in Horsefen Road, Ludham

❶ Leave car park and busy marina and walk up Horsefen Road, going same way that you came in to park.

❷ Turn **L** at end of Horsefen Road, walking along footpath that runs inside hedge next to road. When you see King's Arms ahead, turn **R** up road towards 'Catfield'. After few paces turn **L** on to School Road. Houses soon give way to countryside. Take permissive path on **R** of hedge next to road. Go straight across next junction, following sign for How Hill.

❸ Turn **R** along lane signposted 'How Hill'. Lane winds and twists, and is fairly narrow, which makes for pleasant walking. You will soon reach How Hill House, a sail-less windmill and How Hill nature reserve. There are marked trails through the reserve, if you feel like a pleasant diversion. When you have finished, continue down How Hill Road. Pass Grove Farm Gallery and Studio on **R**, and look for red-brick barn followed by lane, also on **R**.

❹ Turn **R** down Wateringpiece Lane. Pass modern water tower on your **L** and walk past fields. Look for public footpath crossing road. Go **L** along bridleway that runs along field edge until it ends at lane.

❺ Turn **R** on Catfield Road and walk along verge on **R**, where there is footpath. This road can be busy in summer, when thousands of visitors flock to Ludham and How Hill. Ignore lane on **L**, heading to Potter Heigham, and continue walking ahead to crossroads by Ludham Methodist Church.

❻ Go straight across, walking few paces to next junction with Ludham church ahead. Turn **L** along Yarmouth Road, then **R** into Horsefen Road. This will take you back to car park.

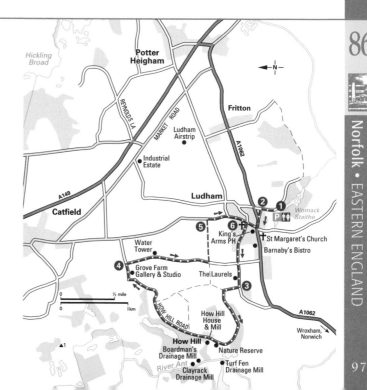

BREYDON WATER Burgh Castle

Vast skies and endless reed-choked marshes.

8 miles/12.9km 3hrs **Ascent** 49ft/15m ⚠ **Difficulty** ③

Paths Riverside paths, footpaths, busy stretch of road, several steps, 1 stile

Map OS Explorer OL40 The Broads **Grid ref** TG 476050

Parking Car park near Church Farm Hotel

❶ Leave car park and walk uphill towards church. Take path to **L** of church, through kissing gate, signposted to castle. After few steps and another kissing gate, you will see well-trodden path cutting diagonally across fields. Follow this to spectacularly grand walls of Roman fort Gariannonum, aiming for gap in middle.

❷ Go through gap, and explore castle, then aim for 28 steps in far **R-H** corner. Descend steps, walk alongside field, and look for 40 steps down to riverbank. Turn **R** along Angles Way and continue to junction of paths behind Church Farm Hotel. This stretch of riverside and reedbeds may be flooded after heavy rain.

❸ Turn **L** towards double gates, which take you on 3-mile/4.8km trail along edge of Breydon Water. Eventually see tall struts of Breydon Bridge in distance.

❹ Pass through gate to enter Herbert Barnes Riverside Park. When path divides, take ⑱ ❽ fork, leaving river and winding across meadow to Broadland Rugby Club, where you climb to A12.

❺ To avoid busy stretch of main road, turn around here and retrace your steps along river, enjoying views of Breydon Water in opposite direction. Otherwise, turn **R** on A12, keeping carefully to **R-H** verge, and continue for just over 0.5 mile (800m) to roundabout with retail park on **R**. Keep **R** on pedestrian and cycle path beside road. After passing entrance signs for Bradwell and just before industrial estate, look for hedge gap and steps leading down to footpath across marshes on **R**.

❻ Turn down footpath between estate and marshes. After 0.75 mile (1.2km), turn **L** on to track for about 250yds (229m), then take footpath through hedge gap to **R**, past farm buildings of Bradwell Hall, to crossroads.

❼ Keep ahead through rusty gate and past abandoned house; follow path between fields. Cross stile and fields to short farm track, which bends **L** to arrive at High Road. Turn **R** and **R** again on to Back Lane. This quiet lane bends **L**, passing houses and Anglian Water station, before emerging on to High Road at Queens Head.

❽ Turn **R** and keep climbing until you see church. Turn **R** into car park.

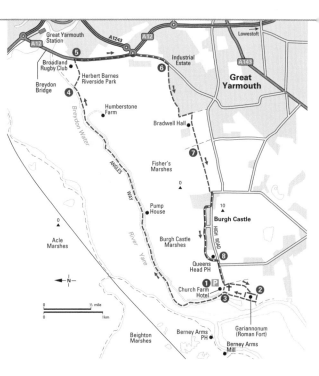

OVERSTRAND To Northrepps

From the coast to the Poppylands.

4 miles/6.4km 2hrs **Ascent** 295ft/90m ⚠ **Difficulty** ③
Paths Farm tracks, footpaths, quiet lanes
Map OS Explorer 252 Norfolk Coast East **Grid ref** TG 247410
Parking Pay-and-display car park on Coast Road in Overstrand

1 Go **R**, out of car park on to Paul's Lane. Pass Old Rectory, then walk along pavement on **L**. Pass Arden Close, then look for public footpath sign on **L**. Follow this alley to road.

2 Cross road, aiming for sign 'Private Drive Please Drive Slowly'. To **L** is footpath. Go up this track, then take path to **L** of gate to Stanton Farm. Climb hill, taking path to **R** when main track bears **L**. At brow follow path towards line of trees. Go downhill, eventually reaching Toll Cottage.

3 Take lane ahead, passing Broadgate Close. At Northrepps village sign and T-junction, turn **L** on to Church Street, keeping **L**. Pass Foundry Arms and look for phone box and bus stop, beyond which lies Craft Lane.

4 Turn **R** along Craft Lane, using pavement until sign marks this as 'quiet lane' for walkers. After 700yds (640m) there is Paston Way sign on **L**. Take this through woods, and bear **L** when it becomes track to Hungry Hill farm.

5 At lane next to farm, turn L. After few paces go **R**, following 'Circular Walk Paston Way' signs. Follow this gravel track towards radar scanner installation.

6 Keep **L** where track bends towards radar tower, following footpath signs. Path descends through woods, passing under disused railway bridge before meeting main road. Cross this, then turn **L** to walk on pavement for few paces before turning **R** along Coast Road. When road starts to bends, look out for signs to Overstrand Promenade.

7 Go down steep ramp to **R** to arrive at concrete walkway. Up to **L** you will see remains of fallen houses in crumbling cliffs. Follow walkway (or walk on sand, if you prefer) to slipway for boats. To **L** of slipway is zig-zag pathway.

8 Follow this upwards to top of cliffs. Car park is just ahead.

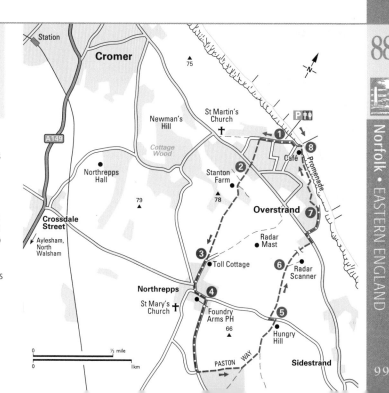

REEPHAM Church Trilogy
Around an ancient market town.

5.25 miles/8.4km 2hrs 30min **Ascent** 82ft/25m ⚠ **Difficulty** ③
Paths Field paths and trackways; beware poor signposting, 3 stiles
Map OS Explorer 238 Dereham & Aylsham **Grid ref** TG 099229
Parking Free town car park on Station Road, Reepham

❶ From car park turn **R** towards Methodist church and turn **L** up Kerdiston Road, signposted 'Byway to Guestwick'. At junction with Smuggler's Lane, take path **L** into CaSu Park. Take footpath ahead, then bear to **R** each time paths meet, to emerge through trees on to lane again. Turn **L** and walk under bridge.
❷ Continue along road to Manor Farm, then keep straight on to track. At first track is gravelled, then changes to grass. Watch out for point near end of field where path takes dive to **L** through trees. Path then emerges on to wide track.
❸ Turn **R** along track and take next turning to **R**, with splendid tower of Salle church ahead. Stay on track, looking for occasional circular walk markers. When track ends at lane, turn **L** and continue to next junction.
❹ At junction, turn **R** by Gatehouse Farm and walk up Salle's High Street to church. Bench in gate for weary to rest. On leaving church, cross road and walk behind 2 buildings opposite church to far **L-H** corner of village green, and turn **R** on to wide green path. Walk along field edge with fir trees on **R**, ignoring footpath to **L**, until you reach end of plantation.
❺ Turn **R** towards road and then **L** along side of hedge. Continue until path emerges on to lane and turn **L** until you reach junction.
❻ At junction, take path under old railway bridge on to Marriott's Way. Walk along this cycle route past Reepham Station, complete with its platform. Continue until path crosses road, and you see steps to **R**. Walk down them, cross stile, and turn **R** under bridge. Walk along this lane to fork; bear **R** to car park.

Norfolk • EASTERN ENGLAND

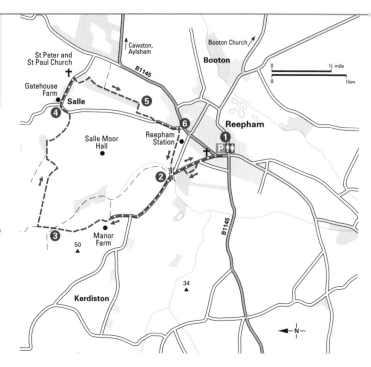

BLICKLING The Weavers' Way

Stroll through the grounds of Blickling Hall.

6.5 miles/10.4km 3hrs **Ascent** 98ft/30m ⚠ **Difficulty** ☐1
Paths Paved lanes and some footpaths
Map OS Explorer 252 Norfolk Coast East **Grid ref** TG 176285
Parking Blickling Hall car park on Aylsham Road (free for NT members)

1 Go towards National Trust visitor centre and take gravel path to its **L**, past Buckinghamshire Arms. At drive, turn **L** signed to park and lake. Keep **R** and go through gates into Blickling Park. Keep ahead at fork and follow Weavers' Way, eventually to go through gate into The Beeches. Continue ahead at crossing of paths along **R-H** field edge. On nearing house, follow path **R**, then **L** to lane.

2 Turn **L** at lane, following its winding path until you pass Mill Cottage, complete with mill pond, on **R** and Mill Farm on **L**. Mixed deciduous Great Wood on **L** belongs to National Trust. Leave woods and walk through pretty Bure Valley for about 700yds (640m) to footpath on **L** (although sign is on **R**).

3 Turn **L** down this overgrown track, with hedgerows to **R** and trees to **L**. Go up slope to Bunker's Hill Plantation (also protected by National Trust), skirting around edge of this before footpath merges with farm track. It eventually comes out on to road.

4 Turn **L** and then **R**, on to New Road, which is signposted for Cawston and Oulton Street. This wide lane runs straight for about 0.75 mile (1.2km), before reaching crossroads at village sign for Oulton Street.

5 Turn **L** by RAF memorial and its bench. Lane starts off wide, but soon narrows to peaceful rural track. Continue along this for 1.5 miles (2.4km), passing through thin line of trees (Oulton Belt) and eventually arriving at Abel Heath, small conservation area owned by National Trust.

6 Turn **L** by oak tree, then **L** at T-junction towards Abel Heath Farm. Lane winds downhill to red-brick cottages of little hamlet of Silvergate. You are now on Weavers' Way long-distance footpath. Pass cemetery on **R** and continue until you see St Andrew's Church (partly 14th century, but mostly Victorian). Continue to reach main road.

7 Turn **L**, passing Buckinghamshire Arms and pretty 18th- and 19th-century estate cottages at park gates on **R**. Continue walking until you see signs for car park, where you turn **R**.

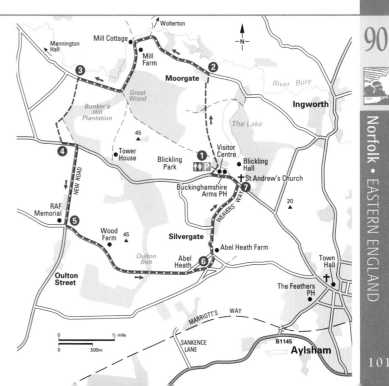

NORTH ELMHAM The Saxon Cathedral

Walk where Saxons prayed and Victorians built their railways.

5.5 miles/8.8km 2hrs **Ascent** 115ft/35m ⚠ **Difficulty** 2
Paths Disused railway line and paved roads, some steps,1 stile
Map OS Explorer 238 Dereham & Aylsham **Grid ref** TF 988216
Parking Car park near Saxon cathedral in North Elmham village

❶ Look around site of Saxon cathedral, then leave way you entered. Turn **L** along gravel track with North Elmham's parish church of St Mary's to **R**. Path winds downhill with hedges on either side to old bridge with disused railway running underneath it. Cross bridge and look for stile immediately to **L**.

❷ Walk through gap beside stile and descend steps to reach disused railway line. Turn **R**, and continue along path until functional railway tracks appear. At this point path moves away **R**, safely tucked to one side. After about 0.75 mile (1.2km) you reach County School Station. Cross road and keep straight ahead, following blue arrows marking Wensum Valley Walks and keeping railway tracks to **L**. Continue for another 0.75 mile (1.2km), past Blackhall Farm, until footpath leaves railway track and descends steps to B1110.

❸ Turn **R** and, at remains of Victorian railway bridge, keep **L**, following blue cycleway signs directing riders to King's Lynn and Fakenham. Walk on this quiet lane

to T-junction. Turn **L** and continue to next junction.

❹ Turn **R** along shady lane, passing pretty Ling Plantation on **L**. Turn sharp **L** along Greatheath Road signposted to North Elmham, to reach other edge of Ling Plantation. Walk along this lovely lane for 0.75 mile (1.2km), to reach scattered houses. Look for footpath off to **R**, opposite track leading to Dale Farm on **L**.

❺ Take footpath to R, mostly wide gravel track. Follow it around to **L** behind houses and then **R**, towards another small plantation. Head **L** into woods, following blue arrows. Path emerges on to driveway to Elmham House and comes out on B1110 by old red telephone box and posting box. This is North Elmham's High Street. Opposite is Millers Old Cottage.

❻ Turn **R** along High Street and walk until you see signs for Saxon cathedral off **L**. Follow them back to car park.

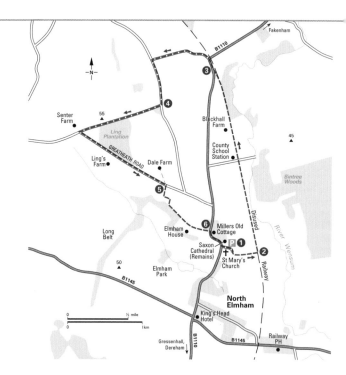

EAST WRETHAM COMMON Birds And Bunnies

Once shaken by roaring war planes, this is now a peaceful nature reserve.

2.75 miles/4.4km 1hr **Ascent** Negligible ⚠ **Difficulty** ☐1
Paths Gravel track and way-marked trails across heath
Map OS Explorer 229 Thetford Forest in The Brecks **Grid ref** TL 913885
Parking Norfolk Wildlife Trust car park off A1075. Open 8am to dusk

❶ From car park go through gate and follow trail marked by green-and-white arrows. This will take you over sandy Breckland heath that is pitted with rabbit warrens, so watch your step. Rabbits can nearly always be seen here. At kissing gate, follow green arrow trail that takes you to **R** through pine plantation. You might notice traces of tarmac underfoot on the route, a relic of the airbase.

❷ Follow green arrows and keep to paths to reach junction of routes. At this point, you could make short diversion **L** by taking white trail along north shore of Langmere, where narrow path leads down to bird hide overlooking lake. However, because the water level in the mere varies from season to season, the hide is often flooded and may be closed. If it is open, this is a good place to observe waterfowl.

❸ Retrace your steps from hide to point where green and white trails converge. Bear **L** and stay on this path as it crosses meadow to reach gate.

❹ Go through gate and turn **L** on to old Drove Road. This is part of Hereward Way and is wide gravel track with fences on either side. The Norfolk Wildlife Trust opens and closes parts of the reserve depending on the season and weather conditions, so it is sometimes possible to extend the walk to Ringmere. Hopefully, you will be able to do this, in which case turn **R** off Drove Road and, after reaching Ringmere, return same way. Look for notices along the road to see if the path is open. The Drove Road will then take you past the memorial to Sydney Herbert Long, who founded the Norfolk Naturalists' Trust in 1926.

❺ At A1075, turn **L** and follow marker posts back to car park.

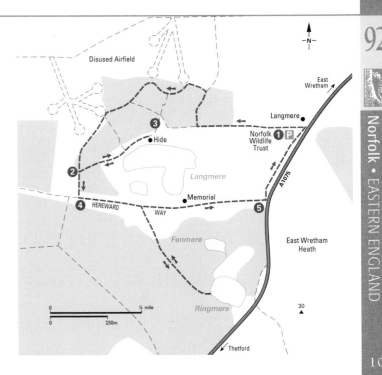

WEETING To Grimes Graves

Travel back in time from a 12th-century moated house to a prehistoric flint mine.

7.5 miles/12.1km 3hrs **Ascent** 148ft/45m ⚠ **Difficulty** ③
Paths Farm and forest tracks, some roads, 1 stile **Map** OS Explorer 229 Thetford Forest in The Brecks
Grid ref TL 776891 **Parking** Lay-by at Weeting Castle, next to church
NOTE This walk can only be done between March and October, Grimes Graves (English Heritage) is
open. At other times, the entrance gate is locked and access is not permitted.

❶ Park in sandy lay-by at sign for Weeting Castle. Walk across meadow to look at remains of this fortified manor house, then follow farm track past St Mary's Church with its round tower. Go through Home Farm, then jig **L** then **R**, passing curious sows in their pens **L**. After walking past pig enclosures, turn **R**.

❷ At junction by Sunnyside Cottage, take **L-H** turn, following track with woodland on **L** and field on **R**. After about 1 mile (1.6km) you reach A1065. Turn **R** and walk for about 350yds (320m) along verge.

❸ Cross A1065 and then follow paved lane signposted to Grimes Graves. Stay on this road for about 1.25 miles (2km), until you see sign on **R** for Grimes Graves. Pass through gate and walk down approach road to enter site. You will need to pay an entrance fee, even to walk here. From car park, follow path to **R** leading across heath to an area of tall trees beside Ministry of Defence firing area. Cross stile over perimeter fence, then turn **L**

to walk along outside of fence to corner of site.

❹ Turn **R** at junction of paths. After 200yds (183m) you see sunken water butt with corrugated-iron roof, looking like house that has half-disappeared into ground. Go straight across this junction and walk along sandy track to A1065 again. Despite proximity of main road, you are in the depths of prime forest here, where you can stand and hear nothing more than the trill of birdsong.

❺ Cross A1065 and take sandy track directly opposite. After short walk, woods give way to farmland again. Pass Brickkiln Farm and ignore track going off to **R**. When you reach end of field, turn **R** and walk along side of Shadwell's Plantation, wood that was planted in memory of poet Thomas Shadwell, resident of Weeting who died in 1691. Keep straight ahead when track divides, and stay on track until it rejoins outward path by Sunnyside Cottage. Retrace steps past pig farm and then back to reach car park again.

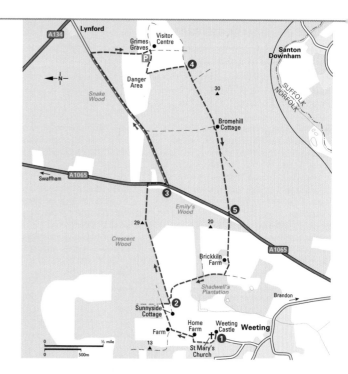

GREAT EASTERN PINGO TRAIL Full Steam Ahead

A walk along an old railway course that has remnants of the ice age.

5.75 miles/9.2km 2hrs 30min **Ascent** 33ft/10m ⚠ **Difficulty** ☐1
Paths Wide grassy footpaths to narrow muddy ones, some steps
Map OS Explorer 229 Thetford Forest in The Brecks **Grid ref** TL 940965
Parking Great Eastern Pingo Trail car park off A1075

❶ From car park, set short way back from main road, take straight path ahead, marked by notice board and map of Pingo Trail. Pass old Stow Bedon station buildings and continue ahead on disused railway line, part of Great Eastern railway which gives the walk its name. Path runs through mixed woodland and after little more than 1 mile (1.6km) reaches farm track.
❷ Turn **R** along track, passing Crows Farm on **R**, and stay on this forest track as it crosses Stow Heath. On reaching Watering Farm, keep walking straight ahead to junction.
❸ Turn **R** along gravelled footpath of north–south Peddars Way trail. You will soon see Thompson Water – shallow artificial lake built in 1840s – on **R**. On your **L** note signs warning would-be walkers that this area is used by Ministry of Defence. Once lake emerges on **R**, look out for sign for Great Eastern Pingo Trail.
❹ Turn **R** into Thompson Common nature reserve. This part of the walk can be muddy, and may

necessitate some acrobatics across fallen trees and through sticky black bogs. There are trails to the lake itself, if you want a diversion to see teals, shovellers, reed warblers and crested grebes. Main path can be hard to follow, so look out for waymarkers. Head for bridge crossing sluggish stream.
❺ Turn **L** after you go over bridge and walk next to stream along pretty path.
❻ Cross another bridge, going away from stream and out into open area of Thompson Common, meadow kept in good condition by grazing Shetland sheep. After you walk through 2nd meadow – in which are a number of large pingos – you will see Thompson village on horizon. Follow track to paved lane.
❼ At lane, continue into outskirts of village. Pass houses, until you see Pingo Trail sign to **R**, just before 'Give Way' sign. Follow it through woodland to return to car park.

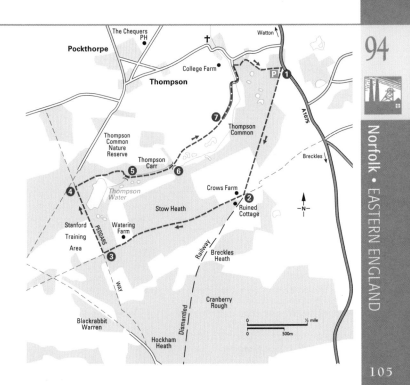

THETFORD FOREST An Arboretum Trail

Walk along the paths of Thetford Forest, from a stag to a mock-Jacobean hall.

4.5 miles/7.2km 2hrs **Ascent** 66ft/20m ⚠ **Difficulty** ☐ 1
Paths Wide grassy trackways and small paths
Map OS Explorer 229 Thetford Forest in The Brecks **Grid ref** TL 814917
Parking Lynford Stag picnic site off A134

❶ Leave car park by metal stag and follow blue marker posts into trees. Jig slightly to **R** and follow markers heading north. Path then turns **L**. Take next wide track to **R**, next to bench, leaving blue trail to walk along edge of Christmas tree plantation. Eventually, reach paved road.

❷ Cross road and continue ahead on what was once part of driveway leading to Lynford Hall. Pass car park and noticeboard with map of forest trails. Continue ahead along gravel path, picking up next set of blue and green trails. Church of Our Lady of Consolation is behind trees to **R**. It was designed by Pugin in the 1870s for the Catholic owner of the hall, but the next owner, a Protestant, planted trees to shield it from view. Shortly, reach stone bridge.

❸ Turn **R** and follow gravel path along shore of Lynford Lakes with views across water to Lynford Hall. Turn **L** across bridge to enter Lynford Arboretum and follow path through arboretum to road.

❹ Turn **L** along road, passing Lynford Hall Hotel on **L**. Walk past building; turn **L** through main entrance gates of hotel and walk up drive.

❺ When you see sculpture of 2 bulls fighting, turn **R** on to wide grassy sward called Sequoia Avenue. Walk almost to end of it, then follow blue markers to **L** into wood. After few paces reach lake. Blue trail bears to **L** at end of lake, but our walk continues straight ahead on bridleway. Path jigs **L**, then **R**, but keep to bridleway.

❻ Cross paved lane and continue straight on, towards Christmas trees. Turn **L** at end of track, then almost immediately **R**, where you will pick up blue trail markers again. Follow these to car park.

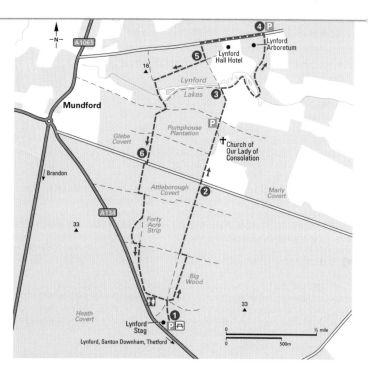

CASTLE ACRE The Priories

A walk between Castle Acre and West Acre.

6.5 miles/10.4km 2hrs 45min **Ascent** 230ft/70m **⚠ Difficulty** 3

Paths Footpaths, trackways and some tiny country lanes, can be very muddy, nettles, some steps
Map OS Explorer 236 King's Lynn, Downham Market & Swaffham **Grid ref** TF 817151
Parking On road by village green, Castle Acre

❶ Walk along lane past St James' Church to entrance to priory. Turn **R** and then **L**, after few paces, down footpath signed 'Nar Valley Way'. Continue; reach pond.
❷ At pond, turn **L** and go through kissing gate along trail waymarked with white disk. Walk through meadow, with River Nar to **L** and enter wood. Keep to this grassy track, continuing through wood to gate. Cross footbridge and keep straight ahead to another footbridge over River Nar, with old Mill House on **L**. At lane with ford on **R**, go straight across to path opposite and walk along woodland track.
❸ Turn **L** by circular waymarker sign and then follow footpath for 0.25 mile (400m) until you reach lane. Cross lane and take footpath opposite (not bridleway on **L**). Go uphill, under power lines and past wood. At crest of hill reach crossroads.
❹ Turn **L** on to bridleway and continue straight ahead at 2 crossroads. Look for deer and shy game birds, and note prairie-style fields to **L** and **R**.

❺ Turn **L** at 3rd crossroads, on to ancient drove road used in Roman times, passing Bartholomew's Hills Plantation on **R**. Keep walking uphill along this sandy track until you see Castle Acre Priory and St James' Church through trees ahead. Descending, go under power lines again, and meet lane at foot of hill.
❻ Go straight ahead on lane – part of Peddars Way. At next junction go straight on again, down lane marked 'Unsuitable for Motors'. Walk past Church Farm on **R** to reach pebble-bottomed river and ford. Through trees you will glimpse splendid views of the priory **L**. Cross river and continue walking along this tiny lane until you see acorn sign marking Peddars Way.
❼ Turn **R** along Peddars Way and keep ahead to sign for Blind Lane. Turn **L** at junction, then **R** into Cuckstool Lane with castle to **L**. Follow grassy path, which skirts around castle bailey, climbing steeply to arrive at lane.
❽ Turn **L** and walk along lane, past old castle gate, to village green.

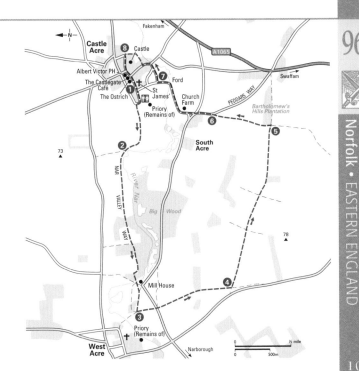

97

SANDRINGHAM A Royal Visit

A stately home, country park and nature reserves on a forest stroll.

6.5 miles/10.4km 3hrs **Ascent** 131ft/40m ⚠ **Difficulty** 2
Paths Marked forest trails and country lanes, some steps
Map OS Explorer 250 Norfolk Coast West **Grid ref** TF 668280
Parking Scissors Cross car park on road to Wolferton

❶ Cross road from car park and bear **R** on lane towards Wolferton. Walled gardens of Old Rectory mark end of mixed woodland. Continue ahead at junction, past St Peter's Church. Road bends to **R**, passing old railway gatehouse and cottages (1881) bearing fleur-de-lis emblem. Stay on this road to make complete circuit of village, eventually arriving at Wolferton Station.

❷ After station, follow road to **L** and go uphill to car park for Dersingham nature reserve and gate beyond it.

❸ Go through gate and take track to **L**, signed 'Wolferton Cliff and Woodland Walk'. Path climbs to cliftop looking out over forest, which 6,000 years ago was the seabed (now 1.5miles/2.4km distant). Follow track until you see 330yd (302m) circular boardwalk around bog to go down steps to **L**. Walk down steps to explore bog walk. Emerging from boardwalk, take sandy track to **L**, skirting woods to return to Scissors Cross. Take **L** fork out of car park and walk along road to A149.

❹ Cross A149 and take lane opposite, passing house named The Folly. After few paces reach lane to **L** marked 'scenic drive'. Turn **L** to walk through gates.

❺ Walk along drive or take footpath on **R** through Sandringham Country Park. When you see a processional avenue leading to Sandringham House on **R**, leave drive and look for gap in trees to **L**. Follow trail past bench and down steps, then stay on yellow trail (waymarked in opposite direction) as it winds through Jocelyn's Wood before returning to main drive. Turn **L** and walk along drive to car park and visitor centre.

❻ From visitor centre, head for lower car park and pick up yellow trail again, which follows main road, but is tucked away behind trees of Scotch Belt. Cross lane, then take road ahead to **L** for 200yds (183m) before picking up path on **R** as it passes through Brickkiln Covert.

❼ At crossroads, where footpath comes to end, turn **R** down quiet lane with wide verges. You are still in woodland; trees here tend to be silver birch. Cross A149 to reach Scissors Cross.

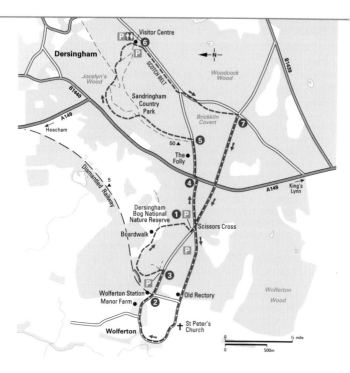

Norfolk • EASTERN ENGLAND

OLD HUNSTANTON Dune Walk

From the coast's wide-open magnificence to a peaceful nature reserve.

8 miles/12.9km 3hrs 30min **Ascent** 164ft/50m ⚠ **Difficulty** ③
Paths Country tracks, lanes, muddy paths and sand dunes, 1 stile
Map OS Explorer 250 Norfolk Coast West **Grid ref** TF 697438
Parking Beach car park at Holme next the Sea (pay at kiosk)

❶ Walk towards sea and turn **L** to head across dunes. This is Norfolk at its best, with miles of sandy beaches and dunes, and lighthouse at Old Hunstanton visible on cliff. Keep close to golf course and after about 1 mile (1.6km) arrive at colourful beach huts.

❷ When you see gap in fence to L, take path across golf course and continue straight ahead into Smugglers' Lane. Emerging at junction, take lane opposite, past postbox to reach Caley Hall Hotel. Cross A149 and aim for road signed 'To St Mary's Church'.

❸ Turn **R** up Chapel Bank, through tunnel of shade before reaching open farmland. After 700yds (640m), turn **L** on grassy track, Lovers Lane, permissive path. At Lodge Farm, follow track around farm buildings to lane.

❹ Turn **L** along route marked Norfolk County Council Ringstead Rides. When you see fairy-tale lodge of Hunstanton Park ahead, follow lane round to **R** along avenue of mature trees.

❺ Bear **L** at Downs Farm and head for gate to enter Ringstead Downs Nature Reserve, one of just few areas in Norfolk that is chalk rather than sand. It belongs to Norfolk Wildlife Trust and area is grazed by traditional hill sheep. This is one of the most beautiful parts of the walk. Follow path **R** through reserve until you reach lane.

❻ Turn **L** into Ringstead, where tower of St Peter's Church stands. Stay on this road as it bends **R** and **L** through village, passing The Gin Trap Inn. Road climbs gently out of village, forking **R** then **L** along Peddars Way towards sail-less windmill.

❼ At last house, look for waymarked path to **L**. This cuts across field, then turns **R** into lovely tunnel of hedges. Note Norfolk Songline sculpture half-way along path.

❽ Cross A149 and walk through Holme village, with its long green to reach car park.

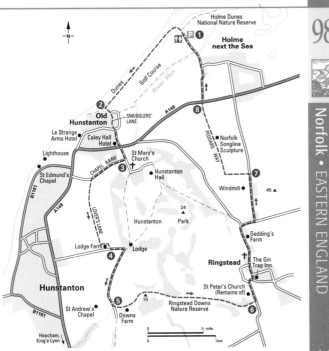

CASTLE RISING A Queen's Prison
From medieval Castle Rising to lovely ancient woodlands.

7 miles/11.3km 3hrs **Ascent** 131ft/40m ⚠ **Difficulty** ☐1
Paths Some country lanes, but mostly footpaths, 4 stiles **Map** OS Explorer 250 Norfolk Coast West
Grid ref TF 666244 **Parking** English Heritage Castle Rising car park (check opening times at
www.english-heritage.org.uk) or on lane outside church

❶ Turn **L** to walk downhill and go straight ahead at crossroads, passing cottages built of carrstone. After road bends L, take lane to **R** between Trinity Hospital and church. Continue through set of gates and follow road around bend, Onion Corner, named after aroma of wild garlic in spring. Continue bridge with white railings.

❷ Take path to **R** through grassy meadow, with Babingley River to **L**. Cross A149 to stile opposite. Follow path across meadow, cross another stile; turn **R** to emerge on gravel lane near Mill House. Keep straight ahead and stay on this lane, ignoring footpath signs to **R**, as it bends **L** to Mill House Cottage. Take wide grassy track to **R** opposite cottage, passing ruined barn.

❸ Track passes through woods, then crosses bright orange stream, stained by iron-rich rocks. Bear **L** across open meadow ahead, heading for opposite corner. Turn **R** here and follow footpath signs along banks of Babingley River. Nettles can be problem, as can boggy ground underfoot. Cross stile by wooden footbridge and continue along riverbank then follow path round to **R**

and cross another stile before turning **L** along wide field-edge track with stream on **L**. Turn **R** when you reach paved lane and follow this to A148.

❹ Turn **R** at A148, then walk along verge on opposite side to 1st lane on **L**. Turn **L** and follow road uphill to Roydon. Turn **R** at village sign into Church Lane. Church has Romanesque south door. Continue out of village until Church Lane bends to **R**, to green-gated lane.

❺ Turn **L** on to green-gated lane, following signs for Sunnyside Veterinary Clinic. On **R** is farm track leading straight ahead. Follow this for about 700yds (640m) to meet another public footpath on **R**.

❻ Turn **R** and follow this sandy track to A148. Take minor road opposite. Oak trees grow progressively larger further from main road. Reach Flowler's Plantation. To **R** is conservation area where native British wild species have been introduced.

❼ Cross A149 and walk down lane opposite to return to Castle Rising. Turn **L** up lane marked towards castle, then **R**, to car park.

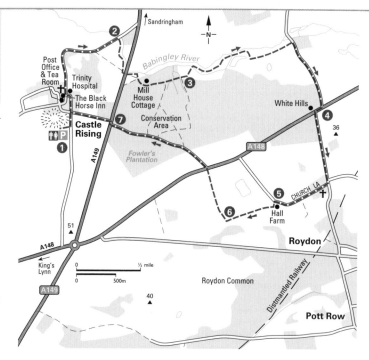

DOWNHAM MARKET Deep In The Fens

Visit a working mill and a floodgate protecting the Fens from tidal surges.

5.75 miles/9.2km 2hrs 30min **Ascent** 98ft/30m ⚠ **Difficulty** 1
Paths Riverside footpaths and country lanes, town streets, 2 stiles
Map OS Explorer 236 King's Lynn, Downham Market & Swaffham **Grid ref** TF 611033
Parking Free Town Council car park in Paradise Road

❶ Leave car park and turn **R**. Reach Somerfield on **L**, cut through its car park to road running parallel to Paradise Road; turn **R**. Road winds downhill, passing White Hart pub, to level crossing and station. Continue past Heygates flour mill on **L**, and cross Hythe Bridge over Great Ouse Relief Channel. On far side of bridge cross stile on **R**. Walk along track to junction of paths by riverbank.

❷ Take **L-H** fork, and cross 2nd stile to reach Fen Rivers Way along east bank of River Great Ouse. Banks have been raised to prevent flooding. After about 0.25 mile (400m) reach bridge.

❸ Cross carefully over busy A1122 and continue through pair of gates to return to riverbank. Path continues until to lock at Salters Lode. Proceed until Denver Sluice comes into sight.

❹ After exploring sluice, turn **L** along lane and cross bridge over Relief Channel. Keep to lane as it winds through farmland and across level crossing.

After passing huge field on **R**, look for sails of Denver Windmill ahead.

❺ Continue along lane for 0.5 mile (800m), then turn **L** up Sandy Lane. Lane becomes track, which you follow until it ends at junction with B1507.

❻ Turn **L** and, after few paces, reach A1122. Cross road carefully to reach London Road, signposted to town centre. Use pavement on **L-H** side, passing police station on **R**. Eventually reach mini-roundabout with Tesco supermarket on **L**.

❼ Keep straight ahead passing town sign, then fork **L** past war memorial and aim for clock tower, walking along High Street and through market square to Castle Hotel. Turn **L** at hotel and walk down Paradise Road few paces to car park.

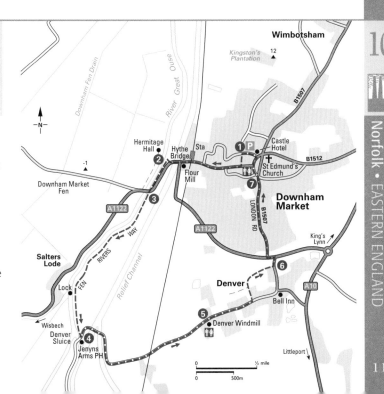

Walking in Safety

All these walks are suitable for any reasonably fit person, but less experienced walkers should try the easier walks first. Route finding is usually straightforward, but you will find that an Ordnance Survey map is a vital addition to the route maps and descriptions.

Risks

Although each walk has been researched with a view to minimising the risks to the walkers who follow its route, no walk in the countryside can be considered to be completely free from risk. Walking in the outdoors will always require a degree of common sense and judgement to ensure that it is as safe as possible.

- Be particularly careful on cliff paths and in upland terrain, where the consequences of a slip can be very serious.

- Remember to check tidal conditions before walking along the seashore.

- Some sections of route are by, or cross roads. Take care and remember traffic is a danger even on minor country lanes.

- Be careful around farmyard machinery and livestock, especially if you have children or a dog with you.

- Be aware of the consequences of changes of weather and check the forecast before you set off. Carry spare clothing and a torch if you are walking in the winter months. Remember that the weather can change very quickly at any time of the year, and in moorland and heathland areas, mist and fog can make route finding much harder. Don't set out in these conditions unless you are confident of your navigation skills in poor visibility. In summer remember to take account of the heat and sun; wear a hat and carry spare water.

- On walks away from centres of population you should carry a whistle and survival bag. If you do have an accident requiring the emergency services, make a note of your position as accurately as possible and dial 999.